DEDICATION

We would like to dedicate this to Trevor Kipling,
a lover of photography and local history,
who was with us in spirit in making this book.

HUDDERSFIELD

A HISTORY & CELEBRATION

LESLEY KIPLING & ALAN BROOKE

THE FRANCIS FRITH COLLECTION

www.francisfrith.co.uk

First published in the United Kingdom in 2005
by The Francis Frith Collection®

Hardback Edition 2005
ISBN 1-84589-208-9

British Library Cataloguing in Publication Data

Huddersfield - A History & Celebration
Lesley Kipling & Alan Brooke

The Francis Frith Collection
Frith's Barn, Teffont,
Salisbury, Wiltshire SP3 5QP
Tel: +44 (0) 1722 716 376
Email: info@francisfrith.co.uk
www.francisfrith.co.uk

Printed and bound in England

Front Cover: **HUDDERSFIELD, THE PARISH CHURCH 1957** H151023t

Additional modern photographs by Alan Brooke and Trevor Kipling.

Domesday extract used in timeline by kind permission of
Alecto Historical Editions, www.domesdaybook.org
Aerial photographs reproduced under licence from
Simmons Aerofilms Limited.
Historical Ordnance Survey maps reproduced under licence from
Homecheck.co.uk

Every attempt has been made to contact copyright holders of
illustrative material. We will be happy to give full acknowledgement in
future editions for any items not credited. Any information should be
directed to The Francis Frith Collection.

*The colour-tinting in this book is for illustrative purposes only,
and is not intended to be historically accurate*

AS WITH ANY HISTORICAL DATABASE, THE FRANCIS FRITH ARCHIVE
IS CONSTANTLY BEING CORRECTED AND IMPROVED, AND THE
PUBLISHERS WOULD WELCOME INFORMATION ON OMISSIONS OR
INACCURACIES

CONTENTS

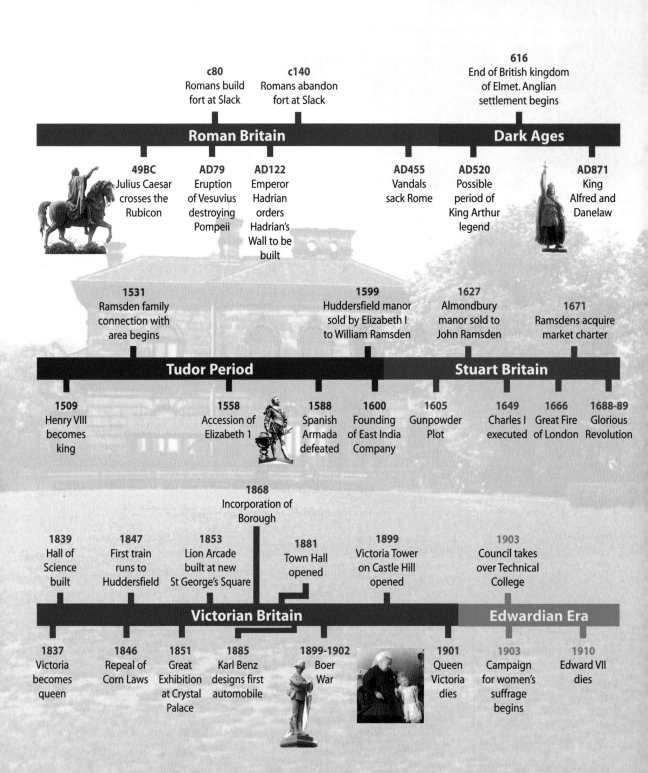

c80
Romans build
fort at Slack

c140
Romans abandon
fort at Slack

616
End of British kingdom
of Elmet. Anglian
settlement begins

Roman Britain

Dark Ages

49BC
Julius Caesar
crosses the
Rubicon

AD79
Eruption
of Vesuvius
destroying
Pompeii

AD122
Emperor
Hadrian
orders
Hadrian's
Wall to be
built

AD455
Vandals
sack Rome

AD520
Possible
period of
King Arthur
legend

AD871
King
Alfred and
Danelaw

1531
Ramsden family
connection with
area begins

1599
Huddersfield manor
sold by Elizabeth I
to William Ramsden

1627
Almondbury
manor sold to
John Ramsden

1671
Ramsdens acquire
market charter

Tudor Period

Stuart Britain

1509
Henry VIII
becomes
king

1558
Accession of
Elizabeth 1

1588
Spanish
Armada
defeated

1600
Founding
of East India
Company

1605
Gunpowder
Plot

1649
Charles I
executed

1666
Great Fire
of London

1688-89
Glorious
Revolution

1868
Incorporation of
Borough

1839
Hall of
Science
built

1847
First train
runs to
Huddersfield

1853
Lion Arcade
built at new
St George's Square

1881
Town Hall
opened

1899
Victoria Tower
on Castle Hill
opened

1903
Council takes
over Technical
College

Victorian Britain

Edwardian Era

1837
Victoria
becomes
queen

1846
Repeal of
Corn Laws

1851
Great
Exhibition
at Crystal
Palace

1885
Karl Benz
designs first
automobile

1899-1902
Boer
War

1901
Queen
Victoria
dies

1903
Campaign
for women's
suffrage
begins

1910
Edward VII
dies

HISTORICAL TIMELINE FOR HUDDERSFIELD

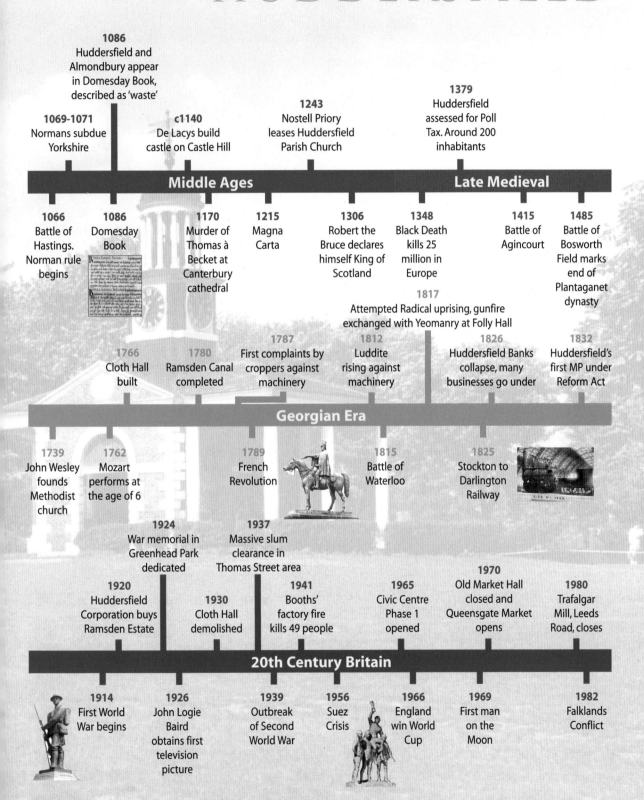

1086
Huddersfield and Almondbury appear in Domesday Book, described as 'waste'

1069-1071
Normans subdue Yorkshire

c1140
De Lacys build castle on Castle Hill

1243
Nostell Priory leases Huddersfield Parish Church

1379
Huddersfield assessed for Poll Tax. Around 200 inhabitants

Middle Ages

Late Medieval

1066
Battle of Hastings. Norman rule begins

1086
Domesday Book

1170
Murder of Thomas à Becket at Canterbury cathedral

1215
Magna Carta

1306
Robert the Bruce declares himself King of Scotland

1348
Black Death kills 25 million in Europe

1415
Battle of Agincourt

1485
Battle of Bosworth Field marks end of Plantaganet dynasty

1817
Attempted Radical uprising, gunfire exchanged with Yeomanry at Folly Hall

1766
Cloth Hall built

1780
Ramsden Canal completed

1787
First complaints by croppers against machinery

1812
Luddite rising against machinery

1826
Huddersfield Banks collapse, many businesses go under

1832
Huddersfield's first MP under Reform Act

Georgian Era

1739
John Wesley founds Methodist church

1762
Mozart performs at the age of 6

1789
French Revolution

1815
Battle of Waterloo

1825
Stockton to Darlington Railway

1924
War memorial in Greenhead Park dedicated

1937
Massive slum clearance in Thomas Street area

1920
Huddersfield Corporation buys Ramsden Estate

1930
Cloth Hall demolished

1941
Booths' factory fire kills 49 people

1965
Civic Centre Phase 1 opened

1970
Old Market Hall closed and Queensgate Market opens

1980
Trafalgar Mill, Leeds Road, closes

20th Century Britain

1914
First World War begins

1926
John Logie Baird obtains first television picture

1939
Outbreak of Second World War

1956
Suez Crisis

1966
England win World Cup

1969
First man on the Moon

1982
Falklands Conflict

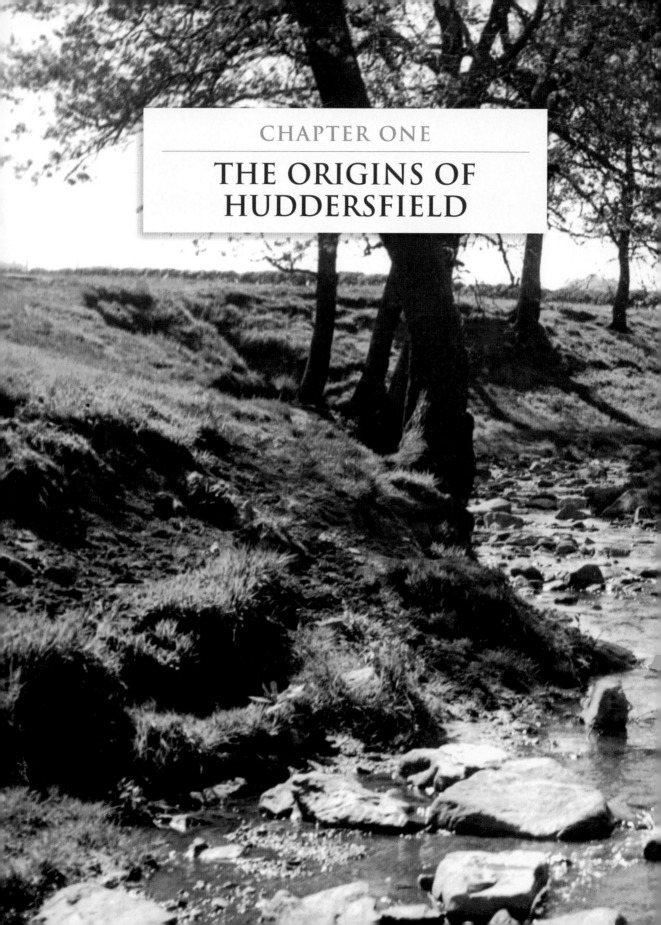

CHAPTER ONE

THE ORIGINS OF HUDDERSFIELD

THE VIEW FROM BEAUMONT PARK LOOKING TOWARDS CASTLE HILL c1960 HI51029

THE 900-FEET-HIGH summit of Castle Hill, a Grenoside rock outcrop, provides a vantage point that makes Huddersfield the only Yorkshire town visible as an aerial panorama without leaving the ground. Describing the scene in the 1840s, George 'January Searle' Phillips commented: 'Huddersfield, with its houses and churches, its chimneys and smoke, is but a dot on the landscape.' No longer. The town has encroached into the surrounding villages and hamlets - Deighton, Birkby, Lindley, Paddock, Lockwood, Crosland Moor, Newsome, Dalton. Their Victorian terraces and later housing estates, schools and hospitals,

mills and factories are now conglomerated into an urban sprawl. Occasionally it is relieved by the green of allotments and gardens, parks and cemeteries and the scars of mining and quarrying reclaimed by vegetation.

As Huddersfield has eaten away at the sides of the valleys, eroding the countryside to the north and west of Castle Hill, even the hill itself has not been safe from attempts to set the seal of modernism upon it. The building of the Victoria Jubilee Tower in 1898 planted a structure which to some symbolised progress, civic pride and achievement; to others, vanity and hubris. But the tower only served to

'At one period of the evening the sun was shining brightly and lit up the face of Castle Hill and the ground in the middle distance. The tower stood out splendidly, with a cloud background which looked for all the world like a range of mountains…'   Alderman E B Woodhead's garden party at Beaumont Park, July 1900.

emphasise the Hill's physical dominance of the town, making it more visible from afar and transforming it into the very symbol of the town itself.

Throughout the 19th century the Hill's focal situation acted like a strange magnet which at times of social stress and crisis drew great gatherings of people agitated by the problems of rapid industrialisation. A tale in The Huddersfield Examiner in 1882 blamed industry for forcing the fairy folk to retreat from the Hill: 'Before the fast encroaching ills, Of smoke and chimney stacks and mills…'. This contained an allegorical truth - that traditional beliefs and superstitions succumb to urban living, technology and scientific education. But the fact that Castle Hill still retains some of its mystery and enchantment testifies that the human mind craves something more than rational materialism. Huddersfield's leading authority on place names, Dr George Redmonds, suggests that the early name of Wormcliffe associated with Castle Hill embodies the sense of awe felt by the Anglian settlers who associated the mound with a Wyrm, or dragon, which guarded such ancient places and their treasure hoards; in this case a 'golden cradle'.

CASTLE HILL BEFORE THE BUILDING OF THE TOWER ZZZ05398 (Brooke Collection)

The dragon connection has led others to more tenuous speculation about place names, linking Castle Hill with Arthurian legend. According to this theory Huddersfield, or 'Uther's field', refers to none other than Uther Pendragon, while the Cambodunum of the Roman itinerary is in fact a scribal error for Camulodunum, the hill fort of Camulos, the Celtic war god and therefore… Camelot. Even the medieval lords of Castle Hill, the de Lacys, have been dragged in to account for the addition of the Lancelot du Lac story to the Arthurian cycle.

'January' Searle, both a romantic and a rationalist, was one of the first to dispose of William Camden's identification of Cambodunum with Castle Hill. Archaeological excavations have failed to reveal any occupation by Britons at the time of the Roman or the Anglian invasions - both Queen Cartimandua of the Brigantes and King Arthur have been dethroned. Asserting the archaeological maxim that 'the absence of evidence is not evidence of absence', some people cling to the assumption that such an imposing monument must have an equally imposing story. But the hard facts we have for the Hill in prehistory are few and prosaic.

GEORGE SEARLE PHILIPS

A PORTRAIT OF G S PHILIPS
ZZZ05399 (Kirklees Cultural Services)

George 'January' Searle Philips, who wrote the earliest (and certainly the most passionate) description of the town and its environs in his 'Walks Round Huddersfield' (published 1848), was born in Peterborough in 1816. He studied for a BA at Cambridge and then travelled to New York. He was briefly editor of the radical Leeds Times and arrived in Huddersfield in 1845 to become the secretary and a lecturer at the Mechanics' Institute. He oversaw the expansion of the Institute into new premises at Queen Street, but left after disagreements in 1854. A poet and philosopher of pantheistic views, he was a friend of Ebenezer Elliott and hosted Ralph Waldo Emerson during his visit to the town. Philips later returned to the United States and, in 1873, was committed to an insane asylum in New Jersey where he died in 1888.

Additionally, little light can be thrown on the Roman period in the vicinity of the town. There is certainly no evidence of civilian settlement and the only indication of industrial activity is a tile kiln in Grimescar Wood, associated with the fort at Slack. Appropriately, this was unearthed in the course of later industrial activity by 'colliers' (charcoal burners), in 1590. Shortly afterwards, Camden visited Bradley and pronounced it to be a Roman bath, but was proved as wrong about this as he was about the location of Cambodunum.

In 1750, the Halifax antiquarian Rev John Watson found a Roman altar in a farmyard at Stainland which he learned had been dug

Fact File

Castle Hill was excavated from 1936 to 1939 and again in 1969, 1970 and 1972. The dating evidence points to settlement in the Neolithic period (c2,000 BC) and the Iron Age period, (c500 BC) when the ramparts were burned. Despite reports of a find of a fragment of Roman Arretine pottery there is no evidence of occupation at this time.

up at Slack. The excavations undertaken by Dr J K Walker of Scammonden in approximately 1824 confirmed the existence of a fort. Part of a hypocaust (an under-floor

GRIMSCAR VALLEY c1955 H151001

Although seemingly unspoilt, Grimscar has been the location of industry since Roman times.

heating system) was transferred to the grounds of the magistrate B H Allen at Greenhead. The Huddersfield Archaeological and Topographical Association carried out further excavations at Slack in 1866 in an effort to confirm that this was Cambodunum. Coins enabled them to date it to the reign of Vespasian.

Judging from the four hoards of Roman coins found at Honley, Golcar and Thurstonland dating from the 1st to the late 3rd century, some civilian settlements must have existed in the area. The Golcar horde came from the site of an earlier find of a quern (hand mill), perhaps indicating habitation nearby. A badly damaged circular enclosure on Lee Hill, not far from Slack, may have been a British farmstead but it has not been dated. The Romano-Britons are generally as elusive as their forerunners. An altar dedicated to the 'God of the Brigantes' was found at Longwood during building work in 1882 (on houses consequently known as 'Roman Terrace'), which shows that some cultural assimilation had taken place. Slack was manned by auxiliaries from different parts of the Empire including the IV Cohort of Breuci from Pannonia in the north-west of the Balkans, whose stamp appears on the tiles from Grimscar and Slack. It is likely that over the lifetime of the fort there was some interbreeding with the local population.

Although much has been done to dispel the myth of the 'dark ages', we really are in the dark as far as the history of the region goes during the period of Anglian settlement. The Huddersfield area was probably part of the British kingdom of Elmet which covered much

of West Yorkshire and held out against invasion until AD 616, but our knowledge of the period before the Norman conquest is limited to sparse place name evidence. On the eve of the conquest Huddersfield was one of the richer manors, valued at 100s. If the Godwin who held it at that time was the man of that name in the Domesday Book (now under the Norman Lord Ilbert de Lacy), he was one of the few Anglo-Danish landholders to survive the campaign of ethnic cleansing and devastation carried out to crush Yorkshire resistance in 1069/1070. Along with all the surrounding manors except Dalton, Huddersfield is still classed as 'waste' in the Domesday Book some sixteen years later. Whether this debated term means literally barren and uncultivated or merely that there was no revenue to be drawn from the land, it shows serious economic and social dislocation.

By the time Ilbert de Lacy's grandson Henry built his castle on Castle Hill in the 1140s, it was probably for strategic reasons arising from the dynastic conflicts of King Stephen's time rather than any need to keep the local population down or gather taxes.

Despite indications that attempts were made to establish burgage holdings in the outer bailey, no civilian settlement arose around the castle, perhaps because of its exposed position and limited water supply. Instead a town grew up around the church at Almondbury a mile away.

In 1288 Almondbury church was valued at £40 compared to Huddersfield's £9 6s 8d perhaps indicating the relative wealth of the communities, and the granting of a market charter to Almondbury in 1294 further boosted its importance. The castle itself had become little more than a hunting lodge and apparently disappeared not long after this, the last mention being to a murder there in 1307. There is a possibility that the keep was accidentally or intentionally fired, since in 1868 the historian C P Hobkirk found a house at Lumb built of burnt stones brought from the Hill by the occupant's father.

Our only indication of the population at this time comes from the 1379 Subsidy Rolls, drawn up to collect the Poll Tax of Richard II. We do not know how badly the Black Death had affected the area a generation before, but Huddersfield is recorded as having 84 taxable adults and Almondbury, 45. Apart from a

CASTLE HILL

During excavations for the Victoria Tower in 1898, foundations for the Norman keep were found. According to experienced masons, these were made of stone from an old quarry on Almondbury Bank along with other sandstone blocks believed to have come from as far away as Ackworth. A five-feet-square shaft cut into natural rock was revealed and partly cleared out, yielding a quantity of skulls, jaws and other animal bones including dogs, wolves and horned sheep. The well was backfilled but was subsequently blamed for the subsidence which caused a crack to appear in the Tower. It was pronounced safe in 1925, but following war-time neglect was closed between 1947 to 1960 to allow strengthening work to be carried out. However, the corner turret was lowered and Huddersfield can now no longer boast a 1,000 feet high mountain.

CASTLE HILL 1957 H151031

Fact File

Perhaps the most famous pupil of the short-lived Huddersfield Grammar School was George Borrow, author of 'Wild Wales' and 'Lavengro'. He attended it briefly whilst his father was stationed in the town with the Norfolk Militia during the Luddite risings of 1812. Borrow describes it as a long low building with a wooden bell tower that he 'mistook for a pigeon house', and about 100 pupils. He also remembered that local people wore clogs.

---

merchant at Huddersfield and references to a wright and a smith in each village, there are no clues as to economic activity. The reference to Symon Fleming has fuelled conjecture, along with the existence of a Fleming House Lane in Almondbury, that immigrant weavers had reached the area and, as elsewhere, stimulated the growth of the cloth industry.

There was certainly a fulling mill at Almondbury before 1200 owned by Lord Roger de Lacy, which may have been on the site of the later Kings Mill. This presaged future developments since it was on the River Colne and was usually referred to as the Huddersfield rather than Almondbury mill. By the reign of Edward III, a dyehouse is mentioned; another operation dependent on a good water supply.

The wealth and prestige of Almondbury is reflected in the dwellings of the gentry, some of which survive from Tudor times - Longley Hall, Woodsome Hall, Fenay Hall, and on a smaller scale, Wormald Hall. It was at Wormald that the Kayes built a school using stone from the former chantry chapel of St Helen, abolished during the Reformation. In 1608 Almondbury Grammar School was granted its charter by James I. It was another two centuries before Huddersfield was able to get one established.

THE RAMSDENS

The Ramsdens's close connection to the area began in 1531 when William Ramsden married Joanna Wood of Longley, a member of one of the richest local families. He died childless in 1580, bequeathing the estate at Longley to his brother John. The estate then devolved to his nephew, William, who bought the manor of Huddersfield from the Crown in 1599. It was his son John, knighted in 1619, who bought Almondbury manor in 1627. Sir John sided with the Royalists in the Civil War and fought at the Battle of Marston Moor. His grandson John supported William of Orange's coup and was created baronet as a reward. After the death of Sir John in 1690, the family's main seat was established at Byram, near Pontefract. In 1584, a new hall was built at the present Longley Park. Longley Old Hall was the last part of the Huddersfield estate to remain until 1976 when it was finally sold. The Ramsdens's remarkable lack of imagination in naming their heirs seems intended to confuse historians.

THE BYRAM ARCADE, WESTGATE 2005
H151701k (Alan Brooke)

Completed 1875, the arcade was named after the Ramsdens's family seat and displays their coat of arms over the entrance.

John Ramsden, (the later baronet), recognised the natural advantages of Huddersfield and obtained a market charter from Charles II in 1671, signalling the end of Almondbury's predominance. Huddersfield was geographically far better placed: it was at the junction of two river valleys, had easier access to Leeds, Bradford and Halifax and was on the trans-Pennine routes. As well as the manors, the Ramsdens had also taken over the fulling and corn mill at Kings Mill with the 'soke' rights requiring tenants to use it and provide for its maintenance.

Exactly when fulling ceased to be the monopoly of the lords is not known, but the rapid expansion of the manufacture of woollen kerseys and broadcloths in the 17th and 18th centuries increased the demand for this process. While hundreds of small clothiers required facilities for fulling, they also needed the means to market their cloth. By the mid 18th century local clothiers were already part of an international trade

KINGS MILL c1980 ZZZ05400 (Brooke Collection)

This woollen mill was an extension of a corn mill on the site of the original manorial mill. In the early 19th century a tramway crossed the river to the wharves at Aspley.

THE CORPORATION CENTENARY PAGEANT 1968 ZZZ05401 (Trevor Kipling)

A WEAVER'S COTTAGE

The importance of the domestic woollen industry to the town was commemorated by this tableau in the Huddersfield Corporation Centenary Pageant of 1968.

that linked them with markets not only in Hull, Yarmouth, Norwich, London and Dublin but those in Leipzig, Hamburg and America, as well as with the woolstaplers who provided the raw material. This was lubricated by a complex system of credit, which, along with technical innovations such as the spinning jenny and flying shuttle, created the springboard for what became the industrial revolution. A class of merchant-manufacturers emerged. Families such as the Ferrands and Inghams of Almondbury and the Whitacres and Atkinsons of Huddersfield not only bought pieces manufactured by independent clothiers but also employed weavers to work up the raw materials provided.

The Ramsdens were soon to tap into this

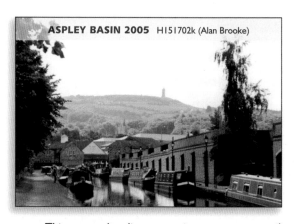

ASPLEY BASIN 2005 H151702k (Alan Brooke)

This once bustling port is now a tranquil leisure marina.

expanding trade, initially building Cloth Hall in 1766 and fourteen years later, opening the Ramsden Canal which connected Huddersfield, via the Calder Navigation, to Goole and Hull. In effect, Huddersfield became a port and the hub of the woollen industry, extending into the Pennine valleys as far as Saddleworth. And it was not just plain woollen cloths which were being produced, but stuffs (worsteds), shalloons, crapes, and friezed cloths and by the 1790s, various fancy cloths with exotic names such as beverettes, swansdowns and toilinettes.

The image of Huddersfield on the eve of the industrial revolution has been unfairly shaped by G S Philips's description of it as 'a miserable village' and Wesley's view of its occupants as 'a wilder people I never saw in England'. But an estate map and survey of 1778 reveals the town's potential, even if it was still basically only a one street town, surrounded by fields and tenter grounds!

The Cloth Hall, an oval brick building which was extended by another storey in 1780, provided security for the clothiers' goods by having windows facing inwards towards the courtyard. It had a circumference of 300 yards and a main diameter of 240 feet. The east entrance was surmounted by a cupola with a clock, making it the most prominent structure in the town after the parish church. A road led from here to Westgate, a narrow crooked street that entered the corner of the Market Place where the recently rebuilt George Hotel stood. According to a later account, some of the galleried buildings used by stallholders, (similar to those in Chester), still survived. Off the Market Place the Ramsdens had put up new buildings which included the Shambles to be used by the butchers who then did their own slaughtering.

THE TOLSON MEMORIAL MUSEUM, RAVENSKNOWLE PARK c1960 H151025

After the demolition of the Cloth Hall in 1930, the Clock Tower was reconstructed as a shelter in Ravensknowle Park.

Past the Market Place, Westgate, then as now, ran into Kirkgate. It wound its way past the huddle of buildings opposite the church and clustered around the Beast Market (the oldest part of the town), down to Shorefoot. Here, on a long 'goit' or mill race originally running from the Colne, was Shorefoot Mill. Probably this was the former Huddersfield manorial corn mill and, possibly by now, also a fulling mill. Below the mill was the area which was to develop as Aspley Basin. Already there was a wharf and Richard Atkinson's new wool warehouse with its quoining, hoist doors and mullioned windows typical of the period, which still survives as flats. Fed from the Shorefoot tail goit was Aspley, or Doodlebank Mill, also occupied by Richard Atkinson and described as a 'friezing mill'. The Atkinsons occupied Bradley Mill further down the river and played a key role in the early industrialisation of Huddersfield.

This detail shows the restored top of the Market Cross bearing the Ramsden coat of arms.

THE MARKET CROSS 2005 H151703k (Alan Brooke)

The George Hotel can be seen in the background of this view of the Market Place.

THE MARKET PLACE AT THE END OF THE 18TH CENTURY ZZZ05402 (Kirklees Cultural Services)

THE VIEW DOWN WESTGATE AND KIRKGATE 2005 H151704k (Alan Brooke)

The Aspley Warehouse alongside the canal, which is probably the one built by Richard Atkinson.

THE ASPLEY WAREHOUSE 2005 H151705k (Alan Brooke)

No longer the commercial focus of the town, the Market Place is now just another thoroughfare.

THE MARKET PLACE c1955 HI51018

ORDNANCE SURVEY MAP SHOWING HUDDERSFIELD AND SURROUNDING AREAS 1888-1891

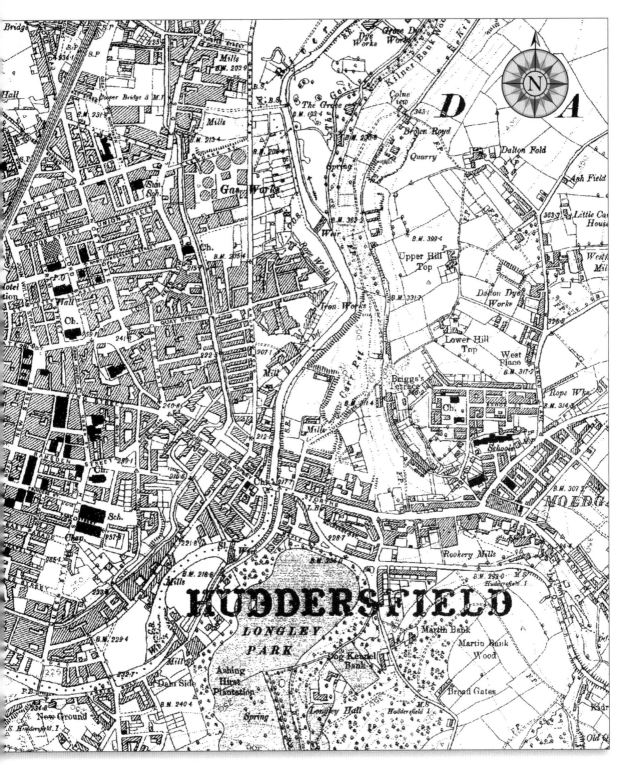

CHAPTER TWO

THE BIRTH OF INDUSTRIAL HUDDERSFIELD

BY THE 1790s, as well as the mills previously mentioned, there were also Kings Mill and Paddock Foot which fulled cloth. The first tentative steps in the evolution of the woollen mill came with the introduction of scribbling and carding engines in the late 1780s. This was the first process in preparing the wool fibres for spinning. The initial twist was then put on the straightened fibres by the slubbing billy. These machines could easily be run by the water power of existing mills and the billy could even be operated by hand.

A deed of 1799 describes the most advanced mill in Huddersfield, Bradley Mill, as 'that new erected fulling mill with the scribbling mill over it formerly in the tenure or occupation of the said Joseph Atkinson and also all those two...buildings one of which is converted into and used as a mill for friezing of cloth and the other into a warehouse, counting house, shops and other uses'. There was also a drying house 'for the tentering of cloth'. Whereas many of the scribbling mills arising around the town in

Fact File

Bradley Mill is on the site of Huddersfield's first woollen factory. The extensive buildings which succeeded Atkinson's original mill have housed various industries including an iron foundry, a dyeworks and a soap factory. The 'Cowshed' of the now demolished Leeds Road football ground can be seen in the background. When part of the mill caught fire in 1913 the rumour spread that the Leeds Road stand had been fired by suffragettes.

BRADLEY MILL 1980 ZZZ05403 (Brooke Collection)

the valleys of the Holme, Colne and Fenay Beck were 'country mills', working the wool for small clothiers; Bradley Mill represented the embryo of the real factory. The Atkinsons had also introduced machinery in order to control the finishing, or dressing, of the pieces they had manufactured or bought. As early as 1787 the cloth dressers, or croppers, had unsuccessfully invoked dormant Tudor legislation to prosecute the Atkinsons for using a gig mill at Bradley. In 1802, at a time of similar agitation in the West Country, the croppers went on strike at Bradley Mill and some cloth finished by gig mill was slashed on the tenters. Two years later the mill was hit by a fire, which an anonymous letter claimed as arson. Undeterred, the Atkinsons not only introduced shear frames, further undermining the croppers' craft, but also seventeen handlooms, showing they intended to control the weaving process as well.

The story of the croppers' failure to limit machinery by legislation, and their frustration which erupted into the Luddite revolt of 1812, has often been told and is a topic that still arouses strong partisan feeling in Huddersfield. Apart from the attack on the dressing shop of the merchant-manufacturer Frances Vickerman at Taylor Hill, it was mainly small cropping shops in the valleys which suffered and Bradley Mill, the prime target, escaped unscathed. The government signalled its support for the manufacturers by making machine breaking a capital offence and pouring troops into the area. Despite executions, the local resistance to industrialisation was not crushed. Some workers concluded that the only way forward was to change the government, by force if necessary. Huddersfield was the only area in Britain where people participated first in Luddism and then in both abortive risings for a democratic republic in 1817 and 1820.

But, inexorably, the 'factory system' grew and, freed from dependence on waterpower, mills were built ever nearer to the town centre. By 1815 there was a mill on Buxton Road/Chapel Hill, powered by a 20 hp steam engine. Water was obtained from a well on the premises and from the canal at a 'trifling rent'. The following year John Sutcliffe's five-storeys-high cotton factory, including the attic and the basement, was advertised for sale on New Street. The carders, spinning mules and throstles were powered by a beam engine capable of 16 hp. As this was reputed to be only the second steam engine in Huddersfield, it begs the question, which was the first? The 'Brick Factory' was built in 1825 to the north of the church, separated by fields and near the wells known as the Bradley Spout. Known for its unusual construction, the mill boasted a 34 hp engine that had originally seen service in Gott's woollen factory in Leeds. On the eastern edge of the town, at Upper Head Row, there was the large factory of Joshua Lockwood, also built in 1825, powered by a large 40 hp engine, made by the resoundingly named Zebulon Stirk of Leeds. This was still working when much of the mill burnt down 89 years later.

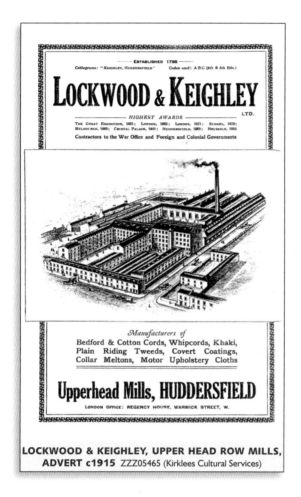

LOCKWOOD & KEIGHLEY, UPPER HEAD ROW MILLS,
ADVERT c1915 ZZZ05465 (Kirklees Cultural Services)

Large mills were also rearing up on the banks of the River Colne. In 1819 the Starkey Brothers began building a woollen factory at Longroyd Bridge, soon to expand into the biggest in Huddersfield, employing over 600 workers. Ironically, on their riverside property stood the former cropping shop of John Wood, where George Mellor and other leading local Luddites had worked. At least the Starkey's left it intact. The Corporation, on the other hand, bought it for demolition in 1891 as the site for a 'destructor' - a rubbish incinerator.

The Starkeys were a family firm who owned their factory and carried out every stage of manufacturing, from the sorting of the wool to finishing and dyeing the cloth. A few hundred yards downstream, at Folly Hall, Joseph Kaye built a mill on a different principle in 1825. Kaye was a builder, quarry owner and brewer, not directly involved in manufacture. His mills were let as 'room and power' to a tenant, or several tenants, involved in various occupations. An advert in The Manchester Guardian the following year described it as a 'newly erected' four-storey mill of 23 by 17 yards, powered by a 30 hp engine, with a supply of cheap coal, 300 yards from the canal, (linked since 1811 with Manchester), and five minutes walk from Huddersfield Market Place. However, Kaye's plans to build more mills on the site had to be postponed. At the end of 1825 Huddersfield was caught in the great financial crisis sweeping the country. The local banks of Dobson and Shakespeare Garrett Sikes collapsed causing a wave of bankruptcies as credit dried up and people were left holding worthless notes.

Conveniently we can pause at a map of Huddersfield at this time, drawn by George Crosland in 1826, providing a view of the growth of the town since 1778. The wealth of the town was proclaimed by the increase in religious buildings such as the £12,000 Holy Trinity Church of Benjamin Haigh Allen of Greenhead, finished in 1819, and the Ramsden Street Independent Chapel, built in 1825 for over £6,500. From Cloth Hall Street, which originated at the main clock-crowned

Longroyd Bridge, formerly Starkeys' Mill, the largest woollen factory in the town during the 19th century, pictured just before demolition in 1981.

LONGROYD BRIDGE c1980 ZZZ05404 (Brooke Collection)

entrance of that building, King Street, the widest and straightest thoroughfare, ran downhill towards the wharves at Aspley. In a southerly direction, at not quite right angles off King street, were now Queen Street, distinguished by its Wesleyan Chapel (then the largest in the country), and New Street, which joined Buxton Road. From the Cloth Hall, Market Street converged with Upper Head Row at the top of Outcote Bank and thence to the Manchester Road. Northwards the area between King Street, Westgate, Kirkgate and Lower Head Row

was a warren of workshops, inns, yards and alleys, including Castlegate, soon to become notorious as the main Irish area of the town. Some building plots and planned roads were surveyed beyond the parish church, but this remained predominantly fields and gardens. From Ramsden Street and Back Green, to the south there was open country between the town, the canal and the Colne, still 'beautifully wooded on both banks' and full of fish and eels. Engravings of the 1830s convey well its rural character.

There was one major problem holding back

the spread of factories locally. Wool, unlike cotton or worsted, was not easily woven on the available power looms. Handloom fancy weaving, the main occupation in many of the villages around Huddersfield, also required an additional contraption on the loom to create elaborately patterned cloths. Although the fancy weavers did not yet face direct competition from machinery, they were hard hit by the financial crisis of the late 1820s and

HUDDERSFIELD IN 1831, THE VIEW FROM ALMONDBURY BANK ZZZ05405 (Kirklees Cultural Services)

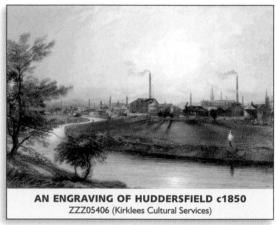

AN ENGRAVING OF HUDDERSFIELD c1850 ZZZ05406 (Kirklees Cultural Services)

SWAN YARD ZZZ05407 (Kirklees Cultural Services)

resented not only bad government but also the speculation and the general driving down of wages that came with industrialisation. Fancy weavers in nearby Almondbury held a series of mass meetings on Almondbury Bank, which led to the formation of a Political Union in Huddersfield. The town became a centre of agitation, not just for the radical reform of parliament but also for the limitation of child labour, in order to curtail the spread of mills and factories.

A Short Time Committee was established which launched the Ten Hour movement led by Richard Oastler. Based in Huddersfield, it came into conflict with many of the leading local manufacturers, dubbed 'the Factory Mongers'. Its main propagandist, Joshua Hobson, a former handloom weaver and joiner, blasted child labour, the repression of trade unions and political corruption in numerous broadsides, leaflets and pamphlets. From Swan Yard (and then Cooper's Court), in protest at 'the tax on knowledge', he published the Voice of the West Riding without paying the stamp tax, resulting in his imprisonment. His short-lived Argus & Demagogue also attacked Ramsden for exacting extortionate canal dues and called (in reference to Gray's Elegy) for some 'village Hampden' to rise against this modern 'ship money'.

The national campaign for the reform of parliament resulted in the far from radical 1832 Act, which still left most people without a vote. For the first time Huddersfield was to have its own MP but, as if to confirm suspicions that the Ramsdens wanted to create a new 'rotten borough', John Charles Ramsden stood in the election. He had opposed a parliamentary constituency covering the whole parish since it would have diluted the Ramsden's influence. His father's agent issued a letter to all the tenants reminding them of the 'soke' rights the landlord still held in the town. At the hustings thousands packed the Market Place in support of the radical candidate, Captain Wood. One flag proclaimed 'Having Long Been Plundered By Ramsden's Canal, We Will Never Be Chained To His Soke', forcing Ramsden to make a discreet exit by the back door of the George Hotel. He later stood down.

One member of Ramsden's Committee was Joseph Kaye the builder. Work had now resumed on the mills at Folly Hall and in 1831 he had just completed another prestigious contract - the town's infirmary. The need for this had been recognised a decade earlier due to the growing number of casualties 'from the extensive use of Machinery.' Kaye himself had more directly contributed to the industrial accident rate, when four of his workers were killed and a dozen injured by a scaffolding collapse during the building of Ramsden Street Chapel in 1825.

Kaye is remembered not only for the infirmary with its sturdy doric portico, now part of the Technical College, but, with some justification, as 'the builder of Huddersfield', including half the dwellings. However, someone apparently had a grudge against him, since in 1834 lengths of rail at his Crosland Moor quarry were ripped up and one of the haulage ponies killed.

THE HOSPITAL c1960 HI51032

Built as the infirmary in 1831, this was the town's main hospital until a new infirmary was opened at Lindley by Prime Minister Harold Wilson in 1967.

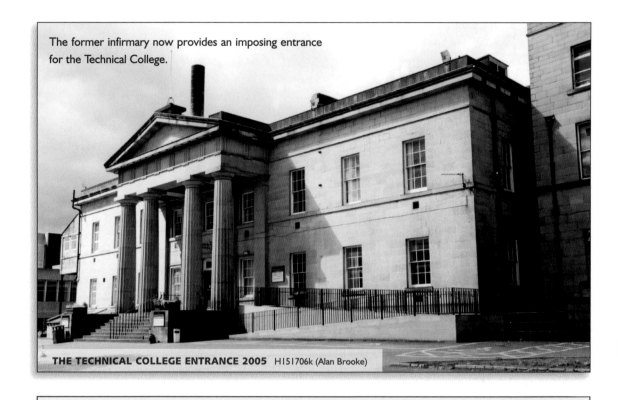

The former infirmary now provides an imposing entrance for the Technical College.

THE TECHNICAL COLLEGE ENTRANCE 2005 H151706k (Alan Brooke)

SAMUEL CLAY

The personal tragedy of the man who made the infirmary possible has been forgotten. Samuel Clay was a linen draper and staunch petitioner for parliamentary reform, almost being arrested in 1813 along with the radical leader Major Cartwright, then visiting the town in the wake of the Luddite rising. Clay was bankrupted by the financial crash of the 1820s and had difficulties supporting his many children, some of whom were deaf and dumb, 'and others of weak intellect'. Despite his own problems, he tirelessly collected thousands of pounds in subscriptions for the infirmary. Just over eighteen months after it opened, he broke his shin while attempting to step over a wagon shaft in the street. Ironically, the injury was not properly attended to and he died, aged only 53.

Whether politically motivated or not we don't know, but 1834 saw the peak of trade union activity which ended nationally in lock-outs and included the arrest of the Tolpuddle Martyrs. Huddersfield continued to be a centre of radicalism, leading resistance to the enforcement of the New Poor Law and its 'Bastille' workhouses, and continuing agitation for the vote for working men, which culminated in the Chartist movement.

Some believed that the only alternative to industrialisation was co-operative production

Built 1839, the Hall of Science was subsequently converted to a Baptist Chapel, then later used as an organ works and a warehouse.

THE HALL OF SCIENCE, BATH STREET 2005 H151707k (Alan Brooke)

or even the socialist communities as proposed by Robert Owen. Joshua Hobson and another veteran of the Ten Hour agitation, the Scottish draper, Laurence PitKethley, were in the forefront of this movement. In 1839 land was acquired at Bath Street, then in fields on the edge of the town, and a Hall of Science built to promote socialist ideas. Of the dozens of such buildings, Huddersfield's is perhaps the only one remaining, and until recently the words 'Hall of Science' could still be read on its pediment.

In 1841 the Brick Factory was gutted by fire, and among the spectators 'one ruffianly looking fellow was heard to express his satisfaction and wished twenty more mills were burned down', but any illusions that the factory system could be halted were dashed

the following year. Thousands of strikers poured into the town from Lancashire and villages along the route, shutting down mills by force in August 1842. The mill-owner magistrates Joseph Starkey and William Brook read the riot act and a cavalry charge cleared the centre of town. Many were arrested and the strike movement petered out, and with it the vitality of Chartism and the hopes of the Socialists. By 1846 the Hall of Science was up for sale, and by 1855 had been converted into a chapel. Two of its promoters were later to become more successful as founders of capitalist dynasties: Read Holliday an industrial chemist, and George Brook a dyer, whose son George Junior built Larchfield Mills on Firth Street.

Despite the depression of the 'hungry forties' Huddersfield's industrialisation continued to accelerate. In 1835 the Starkeys' factory had introduced power looms for woollen weaving and by the 1840s they were also being used in branches of the fancy trade. In 1844 the Leeds Times reported 'Signs of the times - two or three new factories are about to be erected on the banks of the River Colne near to Engine Bridge, Huddersfield and two large ones are now in the course of erection a little higher up the stream at Lockwood…'. Possibly this was not all good news, since one of those near Engine Bridge may have been the rebuilding of Joseph Kaye's six-storey mill, burnt down on 3 June with losses of £45,000 to himself and his seven tenants. As soon as the ruin was cold demolition began. The new mill, as elegant as any of Kaye's chapels or halls with its three pediments and finely dressed facing stone, still stands. In August the following year a mill was being built by Kaye at Quay Street, Turnbridge, on a fireproof principle using iron beams, one of which slipped from the crane and maimed a mason. A fortnight later work was at a standstill as the masons struck against their 'tyrant' foreman.

But it was the arrival of the railway that clearly ushered in Huddersfield's coming of age as an industrial town. The viaducts and tunnels required, merely to gain access to the town let alone connect the lines to Manchester and Sheffield, were in themselves a massive feat of engineering.

The Central Mill was rebuilt by Joseph Kaye after burning down in 1844. It was bought from Kaye's executors by Joseph Lumb & Sons, who occupied it until its closure in 1982.

FOLLY HALL MILL 2005 HI51708k (Alan Brooke)

The cost in life and limb has not been calculated. Bad conditions were made worse when some contractors tried to underpay their workers. It is hardly surprising that the masons on the Huddersfield viaduct thought that 5s a day was inadequate and struck in 1847, four arches from completion. While the hundreds of men who toiled to build the railway are forgotten, the railway station has immortalised its architect J P Pritchett and the contractor, Joseph Kaye. Claiming the reputation of having the most magnificent station façade in the country, its massive Corinthian columns echo Roman imperial architecture and proclaim the triumph of the industrial age.

The station shifted the centre of commercial gravity of the town. As the Cloth Hall had once been the focus and symbol of Huddersfield's prosperity, the Ramsden Estate now promoted new roads and development to enhance the area around the station approach. This new importance was symbolised by the building

Fact File

Five men were killed in the Thurstonland Tunnel over a period of four months in 1846. The following year a labourer was buried by an earth slip in the Bradley cutting and an Irish labourer fell from Lockwood viaduct. On the Paddock viaduct alone in 1849-50 one labourer fell from the crane 'Goliath', another fell from scaffolding, and a painter died while red-leading the iron trellis work.

This is just one of the engineering achievements that created the town's rail network. The spire in the foreground is that of St Thomas's Church, Longroyd Bridge, built by the Starkey family and dedicated in 1859.

THE PADDOCK VIADUCT 2005 H151709k (Alan Brooke)

of a modern and enlarged George Hotel at one corner of the emerging square. The old George, venue for so many meetings and events which had shaped the history of the town, was transplanted from the corner of the Market Place to St Peter's Street, thus opening direct access between New Street and the proposed John William Street.

The railway also made possible another manifestation of industrial triumph, the Great Exhibition of 1851. Numerous local firms exhibited, some winning prizes, like Read Holliday with his patent naphtha lamp, while workers clubbed together to pay for railway excursions to London. The second half of the century saw the growth of the textile and other industries which it helped generate; Huddersfield engineering and chemical firms were also amongst those leading the country.

The growing economic complexity and population inevitably required an increasingly sophisticated and democratic town administration. As lords of the manor, the Ramsden family had the right, granted by the crown, to appoint a Court Leet. The officials, who included a constable and a pinder, were responsible for the running of the town. However, the system was inadequate and by 1816 the people of Huddersfield had a constable of their own.

By an Act of Parliament, on 30 June 1820 a body known as the Lighting and Watching Commissioners was allowed to take over the Vestry and Court Leet. They met at the old George Hotel and were all, by their very nature, wealthy men. This body included

THE RAILWAY STATION c1955 HI5I008

Sir John Ramsden who could appoint three commissioners and also had the right to approve any new ones, effectively enabling him to decide on the composition of this body. Around 1840 a Board of Highway Surveyors was formed which met at the Pack Horse Hotel, Kirkgate, opposite the church. Appointed by the ratepayers (as were the Day Constables after 1845), they were responsible for maintaining the roads. The Committee which appointed them included the radicals Laurence Pitkethley and Joshua Hobson - men not likely to comply with Ramsden, nor neglect the needs of the poor.

THE OLD GEORGE HOTEL 2005
H151710k (Alan Brooke)

The old George Hotel was rebuilt in St Peter's Street. Unfortunately, the taller neighbouring buildings detract from its former magnificence.

THE GEORGE HOTEL c1955 H151009

THE GEORGE HOTEL AND RAILWAY STATION 2005
H151711k (Alan Brooke)

However, there was general dissatisfaction with the Lighting and Watching Commissioners and in 1841 an attempt was made to obtain a Charter of Incorporation, which would officially recognise the town as a borough. Over 2,500 people signed the petition but a small number of the wealthiest inhabitants presented a counter petition and the Privy Council refused to grant the charter at this time.

This resulted in further agitation for a Local Improvement Act, granted in 1848, largely due to the efforts of Joshua Hobson, drawing on his experience of municipal government in Leeds. The new body of Commissioners could only act within a radius of 1,200 yards from the site of the Market Cross, measured from a small brass plaque. Again the Ramsdens were entitled to appoint three Commissioners, allowing them to exert their influence on the running of the town; an interference especially resented since they were absentee landlords, whose main interest seemed to be extracting as much in dues and rents as possible.

Strangely there was some local opposition to the Improvement Act on the grounds that the town was fine as it was. The error of this and the urgent need for real improvement was only too obvious: it was more than the politics of Huddersfield that stank!

Frederick Engels's oft-repeated description of Huddersfield in 1844 as 'the handsomest by far of all the factory towns of Yorkshire and Lancashire, by reason of its charming situation and modern architecture...' usually does not conclude with his quote from a local survey:

'It is notorious that in Huddersfield whole streets and many lanes and courts are neither paved nor supplied with sewers or other drains; that in them refuse, debris, and filth of every sort lies accumulating, festers and rots and that, nearly everywhere, stagnant water accumulates in pools, in consequence of which the adjoining dwellings must inevitably be bad and filthy, so that in such places diseases arise and threaten the whole town.'

Five years later Angus Bethune Reach

AN EARTH CLOSET ZZZ05408 (Trevor Kipling)

'A necessary convenience?' An earth closet, still in situ in the late 1960s.

reported in The Morning Chronicle: 'a comparatively new town, Huddersfield is by no means a well-built town … the more humble portions of the town - that is to say, three fourths of it - are exceedingly deficient in necessary conveniences…'

Filth, animal and human, was everywhere in the undrained courtyards, unsavoury common lodging houses, cellar dwellings and tiny lightless and airless tumbledown houses. Here the poorest were crammed together, many of them Irish, having fled famine and disease in their homeland, scraping together a living as hawkers and labourers. Some sorted rags and bones at home, which along with the cesspits, privies, middens and pigsties added to the general odour. There were only five miles of sewers in the town and only 800 houses drained into these. Some merely drained into lower houses or streets. Such conditions were the breeding ground for typhus fever, often referred to as 'Irish Fever', of which there was a serious outbreak in 1847.

As bad as this was, it was the parish church which was described by some as 'the greatest nuisance in the town'. The stench from the overcrowded churchyard was so bad that windows could not be opened in hot weather. This must have made problems for the vicar who lived close by, and for the various public houses in the vicinity. The churchyard was 'literally crammed with bodies' and before a burial could be carried out, an iron 'searching rod' had to be used to determine where the previous burials had decomposed. There were, as the vicar said, sights to make the blood curdle, with mourners swooning at the graveside, not

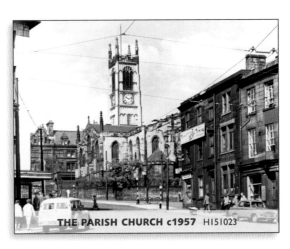

THE PARISH CHURCH c1957 H151023

Fact File

The parish church has suffered from a history of shoddy building. In 1313 the valuation of the church was reduced because of disrepair and although a new one was built in 1503 it was already dilapidated by 1575. The present church was designed in 1834 by Pritchett, (the architect of the railway station), but poor construction has resulted in the stonework weathering badly.

KIRKGATE AND THE PARISH CHURCH 2005
H151713k (Alan Brooke)

KIRKGATE AND THE PARISH CHURCH 2005
H151712k (Alan Brooke)

from grief but the foul air, and grave diggers only able to work fortified with rum. Most of the other churchyards were also full.

Another major concern was the workhouse at Birkby. Again, this was filthy, three paupers often sharing a straw and sacking bed. The food was disgusting, the rooms unventilated and the sick had only other inmates to nurse them. Patients were left for days lying in their own filth and, without enough bedding to go round, fever patients were put into unchanged beds where others had died. Sometimes the living and the dead lay in the same bed. Understandably, the matron rarely visited.

This was the deplorable state of the town which faced the Improvement Commissioners. At their first meeting on 30 August they appointed Joshua Hobson as Clerk to the Board of Works - an ideal choice. Hobson had indefatigable energy, a burning desire for reform and strong opinions which often brought him into conflict with his employers and his colleague, the Law Clerk.

One of his first tasks was to find a suitable

site for the cemetery and to obtain an Act to authorise its opening. It seems that the Ramsdens were also interested in a cemetery and there were accusations that the Estate was only offering totally unsuitable sites on rocky ground. Like scenes from some black comedy, secret visits were made to different sites under cover of darkness. The interment committee denied that the Estate was demanding extortionate prices but admitted that £6,000 had been asked for the Edgerton site; the figure was reduced to £3,554 on a second valuation.

However, the macabre controversies were not yet over. The local clergy argued for compensation for lost burial fees and the vicar of Huddersfield, the Rev Josiah Bateman adamantly opposed the uniting of the chapels by a steeple-topped archway over the drive. One mortuary chapel was for burials in consecrated ground (Church of England), and the other for the unconsecrated ground (everyone else). After a display of very un-Christian rancour he finally claimed victory when a slight gap was left between the arch supports. To the great relief of the town the cemetery was opened in October 1855. George Jacob Holyoake, the famous secularist, shown around in early 1857, described it as a 'pleasant cemetery', and ridiculed a spiritual doctrine that demanded a physical separation of consecrated and 'dissenting bricks'.

THE CEMETERY, EDGERTON 2005
H151714k (Alan Brooke)

The twin mortuary chapels, designed so you can hardly see they are not joined!

THE PARISH CHURCH c1957 HI51023

EDGERTON CEMETERY

Edgerton cemetery had its own meteorological station from the 1870s. James Firth who became registrar in 1876 was a former gardener at several manufacturer's residences, including Woodhouse Hall, Meltham Hall and Lascelles Hall. He was a keen naturalist and astronomer. In 1873 he wrote a long letter to The Examiner expounding an early theory of global warming, claiming that the weather had changed in the last 50 years and that the long and intense snow storms and frosts of the 17th and 18th centuries were no longer known. This was due to the increase of population, the draining of swamps, the railways and the heat produced by the millions of tons of coal burnt for gas production etc. He also wrote on the effects of the moon's gravity on the climate and his meteorological observations were reported regularly in The Examiner. He died in 1895 aged 69. In 1922 the weather station was moved to the Museum at Ravensknowle and the assistant curator, Charles Mosley, was appointed recorder.

This concern with accommodation for the dead did not mean the living went unheeded. The Commissioners had been busy regulating the Lodging Houses to make them more sanitary, but there was still not sufficient decent accommodation for the increasing number of itinerant workers attracted by the economic growth of the town. In February 1853 a warehouse in Chapel Hill was purchased and converted into a Model Lodging House at a cost of nearly £6,000. It opened in 1854, becoming the first municipally owned and run lodging house in the country. These policies did not meet the approval of everyone. A letter to The Examiner from James Brook condemned the socialist delusions and 'communistic tinkerings' of the Commissioners in matters which should not concern them. By now though, the former socialist Hobson was a staunch Conservative!

The cutting of the first sod of the cemetery in October 1852 coincided with the coming of age of the heir of the Ramsden Estate. A public celebration was announced at Longley Hall including the 'Old English' pastimes of a men's sack race, hunting the pig, greasy pole climbing and a donkey tournament. Joshua Hobson and others called a public meeting to protest at the Estate's patronising feudal attitude and the insult to the intelligence of the working men of the town. But relations with sections of the townspeople were to deteriorate even further.

Domestic tenants on the Estate were still mostly 'tenants at will' meaning that they could be evicted legally and any developments made on the land claimed by the landlord, who could also block the sale of such property. In March 1858 this was upheld by a court case, leading to the launching of what became the 'Tenant Right' movement and again Hobson played a leading role. The following year, responding to a deputation, Sir John William obtained the Ramsden Estate Leasing Act, allowing him, if he so chose, to grant 99-year leases. This still did not mean security of tenure and it was said that the town's growth was already being retarded by the reluctance of builders to risk new developments. After another decade of agitation that included an expensive major test case (involving one Joseph Thornton of Edge House, Paddock), and a Chancery decision favourable to the Tenants which was overturned by the House of Lords, Ramsden agreed to the granting of 99-year leases. The Estate's grip on the town had been loosened, but the ill feeling generated lasted for years to come.

The Ramsden Estate still owned the Market Rights, often leading to acrimonious relations with stallholders over rents and this reached a head in 1857. As a result of this, the Commissioners leased the Rights and ran the markets themselves, further reducing the influence of the Ramsdens on the economic life of the town.

As well as these major achievements the Commissioners improved and cleaned streets, provided a police force and laid over eight miles of mains sewers. Huddersfield was also growing in size and economic importance. Unfortunately it was still only one township among others, each with their own local authorities. Agitation began again for a Charter of Incorporation in 1867, led by the Commissioners. A public inquiry under Captain Donnelly was held in the George Hotel in November and Huddersfield became incorporated as a Municipal Borough on 7 July 1868. Its boundaries embraced a much greater area than that administered by the Commissioners, including the townships of Marsh, Deighton, Bradley, Fartown, Lindley, Lockwood, Newsome and erstwhile rival, Almondbury, along with Castle Hill. Of these, only Bradley objected, claiming that Huddersfield merely wanted a place to discharge sewage - a justified suspicion since the main sewage works is still at Cooper Bridge. With a combined population of around 72,500, an acreage of 10,436 and a rateable value of £199,477, Huddersfield was now the capital of a wealthy and vibrant area, making possible civic schemes on an even grander scale.

CHAPTER THREE

A FLOURISHING TOWN

AFTER THE HOTEL the first building on St George's Square was the Lion Arcade, erected by Oldfield & Allen of Lockwood Mills as a cloth and wool warehouse and counting house. Four other firms occupied warehouse space and the ground floor provided retail shops. Samuel Oldfield went bankrupt in 1855 with liabilities of £35,000, including a £6,000 mortgage on the Arcade. Auctioned that year it was described as a 'magnificent pile...[on] the most commanding and eligible site in the flourishing town of Huddersfield' with a rental income of 1,000 guineas. The ground rent on the 60-year Ramsden lease was £159.15s. It set a trend for Italianate architecture which combined practicality with a display of Renaissance grandeur. Oates Bairstow & Sons, for example, in 1873 built a new Fitzwilliam Street cloth warehouse and offices opposite the railway goods yard. Designed in an Italian style 'freely and uniquely treated', it paraded a polished Aberdeen granite column doorway, circular headed windows, a dome and filial and ornamental cast ironwork. To the rear was a factory for their growing clothing business.

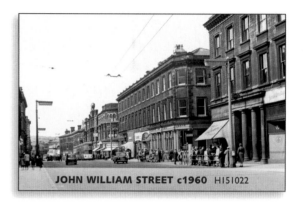

JOHN WILLIAM STREET c1960 HI51022

Little has changed externally except the lion is now fibreglass.

THE LION ARCADE 2005 HI51715k (Alan Brooke)

THE FORMER OATES BAIRSTOW & SONS' WAREHOUSE, FITZWILLIAM STREET 2005 H151716k (Alan Brooke)

The expansion of the commercial area led to the loss of old industrial landmarks. In 1891 the Brick Factory was bought for demolition by the Corporation to improve John William Street. The following year it was questioned why its 'brute of a chimney' was still standing, contravening the Corporation's policy of prohibiting tall chimneys in the town centre. A warehouse for Vickerman & Co was built on the site in 1899. However, the chimney of nearby Newtown Mill, empty since 1876 was not felled until 1909.

While shops, warehouses and employers' residences were rising to the north and west of the town centre, to the south and east, in fields still evident on the 1854 Ordnance Survey map, grew a forest of chimneys under a canopy of smoke extending from Longroyd Bridge to Leeds Road and up the valley to Lockwood. Fairfield Mill was raised on Queen Street South, followed by Zetland Mill in 1854/55. Along the new Firth Street were Gladstone and Larchfield Mills. There was also much rebuilding, as in the case of Folly Hall Mills, where Kaye suffered another serious fire in 1856. Engine Bridge Mill over the road was expanded in 1861 following a fire in 1859. In 1871, in what was described as one of largest fires in Huddersfield for several years, Seedhill Mill was gutted, part of the collapsed wall blocking the canal. Concerned at these losses, E Philips, Clerk of Works for the Ramsden Estate, wrote to The Examiner recommending the fireproofing of buildings on the Dennett Arch Flooring principle. Practising what he preached, the new Ramsden Estate Building on Railway Street incorporated fireproof flooring by Robert Dennett of London. The infirmary extension opened in 1874 also used Dennett rolled iron girders.

However, Huddersfield was not short of its own ironworks and engineers. In 1803 J Shires had established Hope Foundry at Folly Hall and by 1846 Henry Hirst & Co of Leeds Road foundry were making one of the largest castings run so far in Huddersfield, an 8-ton, 36-foot girder for the iron railway bridge over the Ramsden Canal at Colne Bridge. Hirst also made boilers, as did William Arnold of Folly Hall, (later Paddock), and Gledhill, Armitage & Mitchell of Bradley Mills. Two men were killed at Arnold's works in 1881 while steam testing a boiler built for Victoria Mill on Leeds Road. Moving large boilers and castings was also a dangerous task. In one week alone in 1847, two boilers (from Hirst's and from Arnold's), each drawn by a dozen horses, passed through the

FAIRFIELD MILL, QUEEN STREET SOUTH 2005
H151717k (Alan Brooke)

A TRACTION ENGINE 1968 ZZZ05409 (Trevor Kipling)

A traction engine again takes to the streets of Huddersfield as part of the 1968 centenary celebrations.

town. By 1863 Richard Armitage of Turnbridge had constructed a steam traction engine, which was sent on a trial run to Bradford with a casting of over 11 tons - the combined weight of 35 tons reaching six miles an hour. At Paddock in 1864 such a crowd was drawn by the spectacle of Arnold's 'steam horse' pulling a boiler that an oncoming cart crashed, fuelling the Improvement Commissioners resolve to restrict such 'dangerous engines'.

Boiler explosions killed two girls at Dowse's silk works at Moldgreen in 1841 and twelve people in a cotton factory at Aspley in 1857. In both cases the safety valve had been tampered with. Joseph Hopkinson served as an expert witness at the inquests. Soon his firm's patent safety valve and other fittings were on most boilers in the town. In 1861 he built Britannia Mill on Colne Road, to rent rooms out with power from an horizontal engine named 'James Watt'. The boilers were a new design by Hopkinson, improving on the Cornish boiler and designed to run at high pressure.

'His principle object in building the mill was to endeavour to introduce into this neighbourhood what he considered the best form of steam engine and the most economical plan of raising and applying steam.' (Huddersfield Examiner, 29 March 1862.)

Another engineer turned mill-owner was John Haigh, who built Priestroyd Mill on Queen Street South, adjoining his Firth Street ironworks in 1869. The flywheel of the engine shattered and damaged the building. Not a very good advert for the engineering profession!

Prominent local steam engine makers

FIRTH STREET, PRIESTROYD IRONWORKS AND MILL 2005 H151718k (Alan Brooke)

Priestroyd ironworks and mill now comprises luxury apartments and a leisure complex. Fairfield Mill on Queen Street South is in the background.

included Richard Armitage of Turnbridge. The sale of his Turnbridge works in 1873 included various iron and wood patterns 'specially made for the manufactories in the district' and parts for beam, horizontal and vertical steam engines. That year Hirst Bros' new cotton mill at Turnbridge had a new beam engine built by Robert Gledhill of Bradley Mills; at that time the largest in Huddersfield, 'The Templar' could reach over 500hp. Gledhill retired in 1876 after 30 years in business, his last beam engine being made for Aspley Dyeworks Mill.

As well as boilers and engines, engineers specialised in textile machinery. By the 1850s William Whiteley, machine-maker of Lockwood, was producing his patent tentering and drying machine for cloth finishing which, by 1863, was being exported to Europe. He also made looms with improvements in the shuttle action designed by Joshua Crosland of Crosland Moor Mill and had a demonstration model at his own works. Schofield, Kirk & Marshall, of Rashcliffe, were licensed makers of Oldfield's piecing machine, patented in 1850 and given trials at several local mills. It was so successful that when, due to bankruptcy, Samuel Oldfield sold the patent rights in 1855 the advert stated: 'The value and utility of this machine are too well known amongst woollen manufacturers to render any further description necessary…'

Thomas Broadbent established his business around another invention. When it was sold in 1881 the advert described the plant at Chapel Hill as '…specially adapted for the economical construction of the Patent Hydro Extractor, and several machines are devoted solely to this work'.

One of the best-known engineers was G W Tomlinson, the son of local artist G D Tomlinson. He learned engineering at Fairburn's in Manchester, the Armstrong works and Woolwich Arsenal, as well as being a railway engineer on the continent, before taking an iron foundry at Chapel Hill around 1867. However, he is better known as an antiquarian, credited with the idea for the Jubilee Tower on Castle Hill.

RASHCLIFFE IRON WORKS, NEAR HUDDERSFIELD.

SCHOFIELD & KIRK,
Iron Founders, Millwrights,
AND MACHINE MAKERS.

Manufacturers of Power Looms, Mules, Billies, Piecing Machines and Feeding Machines.

BALLOONS & WINDING-ON FRAMES, BOBBIN WETTERS, SIZING MACHINES, &c.

N.B.—We beg to call attention to our Improvements in Power Looms, with two, three, and four Boxes, also to our improved Jacquard. Piecing Machines made upon an entirely new and improved principle.

WHEELS & SCREWS CUT TO ANY PITCH.
Planing and Slotting of all descriptions executed.

SCHOFIELD & KIRK, MACHINE MAKERS, ADVERTISEMENT 1868
ZZZ05410 (Kirklees Cultural Services)

THE CURSE OF CASTLE HILL?

Less than two weeks after his idea of a tower was announced in April 1897, the 60-year-old G W Tomlinson suddenly died. The cause of death was attributed to malaria which he contracted in Venice. In April 1898 work began on the tower foundations. Edward Brook Jnr, owner of the Fieldhouse colliery, subscriber to the Tower Fund and chairman of the Tower Trust Committee, was responsible for checking the progress of the works. His companion in this task was John Haigh of Abbey & Hanson, the architects. Brook also presided at the foundation ceremony on 25 June. Five weeks later he drowned mysteriously in the River Clyde. There was no real explanation for his death and it was presumed that he must have jumped although no motive for suicide was ever suggested. John Haigh continued to supervise the construction until the tower was finally opened on 24 June 1899. About six weeks later, while overseeing work on a warehouse in John William Street, he inexplicably fell from the scaffolding and was seriously injured.

Chemicals production was another spin-off from the textile industry. Read Holliday's works at Turnbridge rapidly expanded from its original coal tar and ammonia extraction into dyes. Schutzenberger, a French chemist and discoverer of a dyeing reagent, actually visited Huddersfield and experimented at local mills, later allowing Holliday royalties on the new process. By the 1870s Holliday had branches in Manchester, Glasgow, London and New York. In 1863 he also ventured into mill-owning with the building of Wateroyd Mill adjacent to his works. Towards the close of the century Read Holliday & Co had also taken up electrical engineering, installing the lights in the new Police Station on Peel Street in 1898.

In 1894 the firm was even attempting to mine their own coal at Kilner Bank, sinking a shaft to the Halifax Old Bed seam and reaching a depth of 115 yards before the boiler of the pumping engine exploded. Few people today would think of Huddersfield as a coal mining area but in the 19th century there were pits right up to the edge of the town. By 1806 coal was being taken directly from William Bradley's drift mine by a tramway, 'to the South End of the Town of Huddersfield and to a Wharf adjoining the Canal...'. Shafts and 'day holes' (drifts) ringed the east and north of the town from New Ground Pit at Stile Common to Lane, Hillhouse, Grimscar Wood, Lindley and Bradley.

The largest mine owner was the firm of Edward Brooke & Son of Fieldhouse, Leeds Road. Their holdings also included a clay works and factory on the site (later known as the Leeds Fireclay Company), which made bricks, tiles, sanitary pipes and flowerpots. A steam engine from the works can still be seen at Tolson Museum. Edward Senior was a fiery Wesleyan evangelist while Edward Junior was a leading local naturalist and Fellow of the Geological Society. About 50 men and boys were working in the pit without safety lamps in 1853 when an explosion killed two hurriers. By 1875 the firm had taken over New Ground pit and were driving a new drift under Stile Common Wood.

A PORTRAIT OF SQUIRE EDWARD BROOKE, PREACHER, COAL OWNER AND BRICK MANUFACTURER ZZZ05411 (Kirklees Cultural Services)

Fact File

According to its builder, civil engineer Robert Morgan, Brooke's Fireclay Works (constructed in 1857) had the highest chimney in Yorkshire and probably the country. From the foundations to the top it was 107 yards (102 yards from ground level), making it two yards higher than its nearest contender in Bradford. In 1873 some coping stones were blown off in a gale. It may have been rebuilt in 1884, since this was the date attributed to the 303-foot chimney felled on the site in 1927 by William Tomlinson. His 17 year old daughter Vera set a woman's record by climbing to the top!

BRICKS ZZZ05412 (Alan Brooke)

This photograph shows locally manufactured bricks including a white glazed one from Brooke's Fieldhouse works.

One industry, minor in economic terms but one that spread the Huddersfield name far and wide, was that of organ building. Peter Conacher was born in Perthshire in 1823 and learned organ building in Glasgow. After working for some time at Leipzig he returned to install an organ, built by Walker & Son of London, at Highfield Chapel in 1853. He liked the town so much that he came back again in 1854 to start his own business, initially on a small scale in White Lion Yard, then at Upperhead Row and George Street. His brother James became a partner but later set up his own firm. A new purpose-built factory was erected in 1873 at Water Street. In 1880 James Conacher opened an organ works in the former Hall of Science in Bath Street, which was sold in 1902. Around 900 organs were made prior to Peter Conacher's death in 1894, not just for local churches, chapels and halls, such as Oakes, Lockwood, Marsden and Northumberland Street but for export to Portugal, India, Ceylon, Burma, Cape Colony, New Zealand, Australia, Canada and the West Indies. In 1874 one organ valued at £1,000 and bound for a cathedral in New Brunswick was lost in a shipwreck off Nova Scotia.

Another local firm starting from humble beginnings was that of Ben Shaw. A former woollen spinner, he was a frequenter of Thornton's Temperance Hotel in New Street, a hotbed of secularism, radicalism and republicanism. In 1871, while living in Charles Street, he began making botanic porter and other non-intoxicating drinks, eventually moving into Conacher's former

HIGHFIELD CHAPEL
ZZZ05413 (Kirklees Cultural Services)

**CONACHER & CO, ORGAN
BUILDERS, ADVERT 1879**
ZZZ05414 (Kirklees Cultural Services)

**CONACHER & CO, ORGAN
BUILDERS, ADVERT 1879**
ZZZ05415 (Kirklees Cultural Services)

**THE FORMER CONACHER'S ORGAN WORKS,
WATER STREET 2005** H151719k (Alan Brooke)

Having survived a blaze in 1910 which destroyed thousands of pounds' worth of almost completed organs, the factory has now been converted into flats.

GLASS BOTTLES ZZZ05416 (Alan Brooke)

This photograph shows some of the glass bottles manufactured by a few of the firms in the area, including a rare intact Ben Shaw's 'Codd Bottle'.

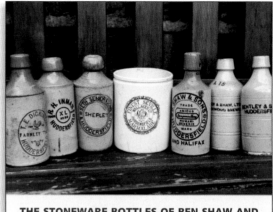

THE STONEWARE BOTTLES OF BEN SHAW AND OTHER LOCAL BREWERS ZZZ05417 (Alan Brooke)

works at Upperhead Row. He was a founder of the Yorkshire Association of Mineral Water Manufacturers and was instrumental in establishing the National Union Bottle Exchange in Huddersfield, where 'stray bottles' were collected for return to their owners. The motto on his own bottles was 'Amicus Humani Generis' - Friend of the Human Race. In 1895 he moved to Willow Lane at Birkby which is still the site of a soft drinks bottling plant.

Following the death of Joseph Kaye in 1858, no one person emerged to claim his title of the builder of Huddersfield. The nearest contender was Abraham Graham who, like Kaye, was also a quarry owner. His contracts included mill buildings (such as Hirst Bros' cotton mill at Turnbridge in 1873), Somerset Bridge at Aspley, the George Hotel extension, the Town Hall, the High Street Methodist church, Milton church, and the Mill Hill Sanitorium. A year before his

BEN SHAW, PRODUCTS ADVERT 1879 ZZZ05418
(Kirklees Cultural Services)

death in 1899 he was one of the prime movers in opening the Builders Exchange Club on Wood Street, along with a fellow contractor and the then mayor Alderman W H Jessop. The club was a place where employers could discuss issues such as labour problems, as well as wheeling and dealing over contracts. Graham was not only a mason by trade. Like many others in the town's hierarchy he was also a Freemason.

Several prestigious contracts were also carried out by the firm of Benjamin Graham & Sons, Folly Hall, including work for the Ramsden Estate on buildings designed by Huddersfield-born architect W H Crossland. These included contracts for the Estate Buildings (1868-1874), Byram Buildings (1870-1875) and alterations to Longley Hall (1871-1875), but the Castle Hill Tower (1898-1899) was undoubtedly, the firm's highest profile project.

The building boom gave the operative masons bargaining power. In 1860 they went on strike for a nine-hour day, bringing building throughout the town to a standstill. The following year, the masons' labourers went on strike against an attempted wage reduction, leading to an assault on blacklegs and three years in gaol for one striker. In 1867 the masons struck, demanding 30s a week and a decade later for 32s for a 49-hour week. There were disputes in 1879 (on the new Market Hall), in 1892 and again in 1897 when skilled masons were in high demand.

The expansion of the town was only possible because of the infrastructure provided by municipal organisation and investment; the Borough Council built on the achievements of the Improvement Commissioners.

The first mayor of the new borough from 1868 to 1871 was Charles Henry Jones. Originally from Buxton, he liked to recount the story of how as a young man, staying at an inn in the Delamere Forest, he was forced to bar his door against a rowdy drunken troop of the Cheshire Yeomanry, fresh from the massacre at Peterloo. Animosity still lingered from the Tenant Right controversy and Jones refused to wear the mayorial chain presented by Sir John Ramsden. However he denied that he had referred to it as a 'gewgaw' and 'bauble', or suggested that it should be melted down. Apart from his political objections he was also an austere man, a stalwart of Ramsden Street Chapel with a dislike of ostentation. But this didn't stop him, according to Joshua Hobson, 'guttling and guzzling' at a banquet at the George Hotel.

The Town Council initially met at the former Philosophical Hall (called the Theatre Royal since 1866), between Ramsden Street and Bull and Mouth Street, which had been built in the 1830s for the Literary and Philosophical Society. This burnt down in 1880 during the run of a play called 'Drink' but its pawnbroker-owner, Mr Love, built a new theatre on the site. However, the Corporation had already moved to purpose built offices on the site of John Cook's warehouse and timber yard, a part of the building now referred to as the Town Hall. In fact, this was one of two buildings (and little was done to hide the fact): the Municipal Offices opened in 1878

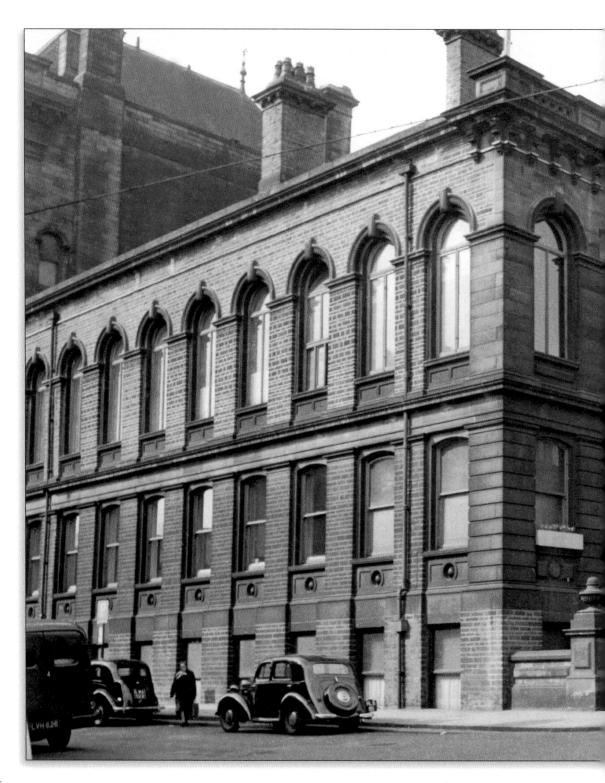

THE TOWN HALL c1955 HI51012

and in 1881 the Public, or Concert, Hall, in a more elaborate style was completed. Its beautiful internal ornamentation cost more than money. Whilst decorating the ceiling, a 27-year-old paper hanger and painter, Stephen Llewellyn Whittard, fell to his death from the scaffold. He died leaving a wife and four young children.

At the opening ceremony, Mayor Thomas Denham described the vast improvements he had witnessed in Huddersfield and paid tribute to the 'cordial relations' which now existed between the Corporation and the Ramsden Estate office under Major Graham. Some ratepayers opposed any Town Hall as an unnecessary expense. The Chamber of Commerce supported one, but thought this was 'inconveniently situated away from the centre in a narrow and confined space, bounded on one side by a row of squalid hovels … utterly inadequate and derogatory to the dignity of the town. By facing Princess Street, it gave the impression, as one paper reported in a slightly puzzled way, that 'the front is at the back,' a conundrum which has continued to puzzle townspeople and visitors alike over the years. Handel's head looks down from the main entrance, appropriately enough, considering the world famous performances of his Messiah by Huddersfield Choral Society. The hall's London-made organ was bought from the Albert Hall Company of Newport and rebuilt by James Conacher & Sons. The hall's acoustics, whether by accident or clever design, are excellent.

The architect and Borough Surveyor, John Henry Abbey of Lockwood, did not

THE TOWN HALL 2005 H151720k (Alan Brooke)

This photograph shows the main entrance to the concert hall. Although bereft of its original ornate wrought iron canopy the 'front entrance at the back' is still impressive. The other heads, carved by a Thomas Stocks of Berry Brow, include Shakespeare, Isaac Newton, James Watt and William Hogarth.

live to see the work completed. A surveyor for 25 years, first with the Improvement Commissioners, he died in November 1880. Although most of his work was more mundane, it was practical. He oversaw some of the main improvements in the town, including the widening and straightening of the approaches at Somerset Bridge and Engine Bridge, as well as new sewers. Just before his death he was working on plans for the new tramway system. Another of his buildings still standing is the

Mechanics' Institute at Lockwood.

In 1876 the Corporation bought up the market rights and tolls for £14,453 from Ramsden from whom they had previously leased. Plans were made to build a Market Hall worthy of the town. The site chosen

THE SHAMBLES c1875
ZZZ05419 (Kirklees Cultural Services)

was the Shambles. Previously known as the Pig Market, it was a place for slaughtering and selling meat and where there were now rows of butchers' shops. This was purchased from Ramsden for £6,491. Designed by local architect Edward Hughes of Lord Street, the foundation stone for the Market Hall was laid on 5 September 1878 and was completed in March 1880 at a cost of £31,325. Described as geometrical, or decorated Gothic, withan imposing clock tower, it was of 'elegant appearance' and the Chamber of Commerce claimed it to be an 'ornament to the town'. But, even before it opened, critics complained: 'It's a beautiful building, but it's too small'.

KING STREET c1960 H151019

In the centre of the picture is the Market Hall in all its gothic splendour. Its destruction in 1970 is now lamented since, with imaginative refurbishment, it could have continued to serve as 'an ornament to the town'.

MARKET HALL, DETAIL ZZZ05441 (Trevor Kipling)

THE MARKET HALL, INTERIOR 1969
ZZZ05439 (Trevor Kipling)

This view of the interior of the hall shows the lattice and girder ironwork of the roof.

Fact File

Edward Hughes was also the designer of the Huddersfield Banking Company offices at the junction of New Street and Cloth Hall Street. Started in 1880 and subsequently described as a 'somewhat free treatment of the Renaissance', it was perhaps the town's most idiosyncratic and baroque building with its distinctive copper onion dome. Both of Hughes's architectural gems shared the same fate less than a century after their construction.

Slaughtering for the Shambles had been done in an old building at Aspley in 'most unfavourable conditions'. The sum of £1,343 was paid to the Estate in compensation for its abolition and in 1877 land, at a cost of a further £16,115, was bought for a new cattle market and slaughter house at Great Northern Street. A modern cold storage building was attached to the slaughterhouse in 1900 built of local stone by A Graham & Co and was 'exclusive of superfluous architectural embellishment'. The machinery was installed by the Lind British Refrigeration Co.

One of the first acts of the council in 1869 was to purchase the waterworks from the Waterworks Commissioners. The main supply at this time was from reservoirs at Longwood fed to a tank at Spring Street, where the Waterworks building of 1828 can still be seen. The construction of new reservoirs were soon begun to ensure adequate supplies of

Hughes's Huddersfield Banking Company offices can be seen on the left of the photograph.

NEW STREET c1955 H151016

CLOTH HALL

While the Market Hall was under construction, the Cloth Hall served as a temporary market. Although further enlarged in 1863, its original purpose became redundant with the demise of the small clothiers and the fact that mainstream manufacturers now had warehouses and commercial travellers to sell their cloth. The Chamber of Commerce discussed the possible purchase of the hall with the Ramsden Estate in 1880, in order to build a Commercial Exchange on the site. In turn, the Estate cashier, Isaac Horden, proposed using it to house all the various traders still cluttering the streets under one roof. It was reopened on 1 January 1881 with an Exchange (in the central avenue), a Reading Room (in the South Transept) and a Council Room for Chamber of Commerce meetings. The circular part was converted into offices for Exchange users and 'Proper accommodation has also been provided in connection with the lavatory'. It formally closed on 31 December 1929.

clean water for the expanded Borough and outlying districts. In 1870 work commenced at Deerhill, followed by Blackmoorfoot; both schemes had already been planned by the Waterworks Commissioners. In February and March 1872 work was interrupted by a navvies' strike. The police

were called out in force but there were no incidents and all but 60 men simply left for other jobs. The reservoirs were finally completed in 1876. In August 1873 the first water from springs at Wessenden was being piped to Huddersfield and by 1881 the reservoir at Wessenden Head was finished.

NEW STREET c1955 H151016

THE FORMER WATERWORKS COMMISSIONERS' OFFICES
BUILT 1828, SPRING STREET 2005 HI51721k (Alan Brooke)

Bank Bottom Mill at Marsden was bought in 1887 by Huddersfield Corporation for £9,000, as it lay near the proposed Butterley reservoir embankment, in a formerly 'sheltered and beautifully wooded dell'.

In 1871 the Council purchased Huddersfield Gas Company's works and in 1874 the Moldgreen gasworks. The Gas Committee later branched out into the generation of municipal electricity when land near the gasworks in St Andrew's Road was chosen for a generator, which in July 1893 supplied 38 consumers with electric lighting, including the Town Hall, Market Hall and Technical School.

In the early 1880s Huddersfield Corporation also pioneered municipal housing with the construction of 160 terraced houses at Turnbridge under the Artisans Dwellings Act. Near to the Read Holliday Chemical Works and several mills and workshops, they were not in a very salubrious setting; a fact belied by the charmingly named Hope Street, Rose Street, Lily Street and other similarly named roads. In 1903 there were plans to build 69 'artisans' dwellings' at Aspley requiring the demolition of four chimneys, the most famous being the one belonging to the long abandoned Dewhirst woollen cloth print works. John Tinker & Sons of Manchester Road felled the 45-yards-high, 1,200-tons chimney by the pit prop and fire method, used until recently by the late Fred Dibnah. It was a popular spectacle even then, attracting a large crowd and several 'disciples of Kodak'.

TURNBRIDGE, ARTISANS' DWELLINGS c1960
ZZZ05420 (Kirklees Cultural Services)

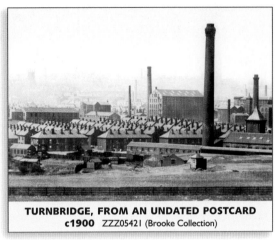

TURNBRIDGE, FROM AN UNDATED POSTCARD
c1900 ZZZ05421 (Brooke Collection)

This image depicts the archetypal northern mill town scene of terraced houses clustered around a mill. In fact this was not a feature of Huddersfield until the late 19th century and in this instance the development of the dwellings was not related to the mill.

In the 1870s the Corporation had tried to reduce pollution in the town by clamping down on 'the smoke nuisance'. If dense smoke was seen to be emitting for an unreasonable period of time, both the boiler stoker and the owner could be prosecuted. Dewhirst had been one of the culprits in 1874, when the judge commented it was unfair that manufacturers should be liable for the stoker's negligence. It was apparently not regarded unfair that stokers could be fined when the equipment or coal was at fault. By the 1890s several mills were experimenting with Hinchliffe's Patent Smoke Consumers, manufactured at Paddock. One of the best known 'Nuisance Inspectors' was W R Croft, a leading local radical and historian, who published a history of Oastler and the Factory Movement in 1888.

In March 1873, two years after the Local Government Board had been established, John Benson Pritchett, (son of the railway station's architect), was appointed to the newly created post of Medical Officer of Health. His reports show that although conditions had improved since the 1840s, there was still bad housing and sanitation with the ensuing health problems. Two of the borough's water supplies were badly polluted. One supply flowing from Sheepridge to Fartown received drainage which contained animal and human urine and excrement: from a house, a pub, a mistal (cowhouse), stables, several cottages and the road. He banned its use and ordered the consumers to rely on the new Corporation supplies.

Pritchett gave practical examples of the dangers of infectious diseases. In one case, at Upperhead Row, a girl with smallpox was sharing a room with her parents where her father was making ginger beer for sale in pubs! A special clause was inserted into the new Improvement Act 1876 requiring that all doctors must inform the MOH of any infectious diseases in their area, making Huddersfield one of the first authorities to enforce what only became national law in 1889.

Pritchett was also concerned about the infant mortality rate and attributed it to the large number of working mothers and the inadequacy of childcare. His successor, Dr James Moore, and Alderman Benjamin 'Baby' Broadbent continued his work by educating women in the merits of breastfeeding and cleanliness. They introduced a byelaw reducing the 42-day limit for birth registration so that checks could be made on mothers and babies - another first for Huddersfield which became national law a year later. Despite opposition they also introduced a voluntary scheme for mothers to register pregnancies and receive prenatal care - long before prenatal clinics were established. Consequently, between 1877 and 1914 there was a 60% fall in the mortality rate of under-fives. Alderman Broadbent received recognition for his pioneering work in 1918 when he was made a Freeman of the Borough. By the turn of the century Huddersfield had one of the lowest child mortality rates and incidences of infectious diseases in the country.

The Corporation's most original innovation came in 1880 when they secured an Act enabling them to construct a tramway, becoming the first local authority to municipalize public transport. However, it was partly by accident that the Corporation ran the system rather than simply laying the lines - no outside company wanted the contract. The first trams were steam powered

and the former theatre/circus site in Lord Street (now the site of the Wholesale Market) was purchased for a tram shed. The trial run, with the Board of Trade inspector on board, was to Dungeon Wood and back on 16 November 1882. The journey down Chapel Hill through Lockwood to the terminus was entirely satisfactory. On the return journey the fully laden tram was running well until ordered by the inspector to stop and restart on Chapel Hill - the steepest tramway gradient in England. It was a foggy day, the tracks were slippery and the tram refused to move until 25 passengers had alighted. On reaching Buxton Road it was found that the brake had been on ever since it left Lockwood. A repeat performance, minus brake, proved a success.

The first route from Lockwood to Fartown commenced on 11 January 1883 and the service was gradually extended. Public confidence was shaken on 3 July when a tram on the Lindley route ran out of control. Running at high speed down Trinity Street, it crashed at the left turn into Railway Street, injuring 28 people and killing seven. With more trams operating, the depot was moved to a larger site at Great Northern Street. By 1887 they had added the profitable service of delivering parcels between shops on the route and in 1893 even added letterboxes, emptied every hour by the Postal Authorities.

By 1900 routes were extended beyond the Borough to Linthwaite, Slaithwaite and, by 1902, Honley. This encouraged the introduction of more efficient electric trams and, the building of a depot and power station at Longroyd Bridge. Public transport was a

THE LION ARCADE c1895 ZZZ05422 (Kirklees Cultural Services)

A steam tram can be seen passing the Britannia Building towards the right hand side of the photograph.

great boon to the working classes, allowing them to travel further and more cheaply to work, especially after the concession of working men's fares. With the controversial introduction of Sunday trams, they also offered new opportunities for leisure.

One popular resort was Beaumont Park. The first sod was cut on land donated by Henry Frederick Beaumont of Whitley Hall at Dungeon Wood in May 1880. Its opening by the Duke and Duchess of Albany in October 1883 was the occasion of the first royal visit to Huddersfield. The breaking up of the wood destroyed one of the last local refuges of the blindworm and several rare plants and not everyone was happy with the environmental damage. 'Disgust' in a letter to The Examiner attacked a new

bridge feature as a 'hideosity ... the climax of the ostentatious and costly vulgarity, which has transformed a spot, which nature meant to be beautiful and had made it so, into a blotch of ugliness, a memorial for times to come of the destructive folly and constructive conceit of the powers that were in Huddersfield in the years 1882-84'. Local naturalists were mollified somewhat by the provision of a Botanical Garden plot for wild flowers and herbs - until trippers started digging up the specimens.

Two miles outside of Huddersfield, in relatively unspoilt countryside, Beaumont Park did not provide the basic function of an urban public green space. Greenhead Park was to assume this role after a long struggle mainly by one man, Alderman Thomas

BEAUMONT PARK c1960 HI51043

The neat flowerbeds and manicured lawns were carved out of the wild Dungeon Wood in what some people even then considered an act of environmental vandalism.

Denham, a stalwart of Highfields Chapel. As early as 1869 he called a public meeting to win support for the acquisition of the Greenhead estate, including Gledholt Glen (now known as T P Woods after former owner, T P Crosland), to prevent the encroachment of housing. Both the mayor, C H Jones, and the town clerk opposed the purchase. The Ramsden Estate was demanding too high a price and would benefit from the new roads by building houses on the parts they refused to sell. Denham was so committed to this project that he rented the land himself from the Ramsden Estate and by 1872 had opened it to the public in the summer for concerts, fetes and other gatherings. It was eventually purchased by the Borough for £30,000 and officially opened on 27 September 1884.

THOMAS DENHAM.

A PORTRAIT OF ALDERMAN THOMAS DENHAM
ZZZ05423 (Kirklees Cultural Services)

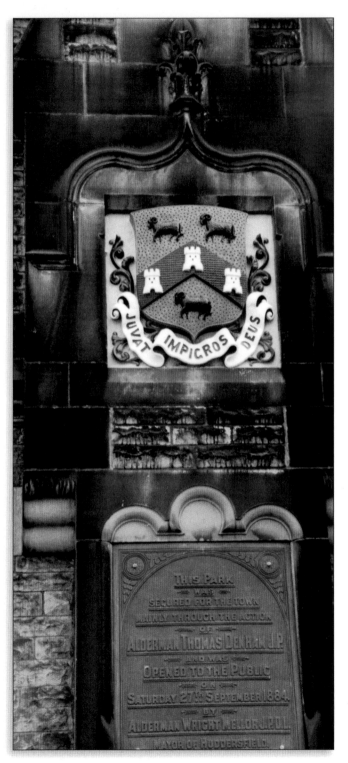

A PLAQUE IN GREENHEAD PARK 2005
H151722k (Alan Brooke)

The plaque commemorates the opening of the park and Alderman Denham's efforts and is surmounted with the Borough coat of arms.

The achievements of Huddersfield Corporation touched many aspects of people's lives, undoubtedly for the better and to an extent seen in few other places. The Yorkshire Factory Times claimed in 1896: 'in fact, 99 per cent of the towns and cities are behind Huddersfield in municipal enterprise … Huddersfield is one of those places which has done things of a communistic character and not known it … the Corporation is the biggest employer of labour and property owner in the borough'.

Local historian and ex-councillor D F E Sykes agreed. Although only one or two socialists had sat on the council, it had 'from the first acted on the main lines of a well-considered, just and practical socialism'. A claim many of the ratepayers - and most of the councillors - would have been mortified to hear!

GREENHEAD PARK c1960 HI51035

D F E SYKES

D F E Sykes, the writer of the first comprehensive history of Huddersfield, published in 1898, had a turbulent career. He established a flourishing business as a solicitor in the town in 1877 and became a Liberal councillor in 1880. His radical views led him to publish a short lived newspaper, The Northern Pioneer, and in 1883 he supported the weavers during their bitter ten week strike, speaking at the great mass meeting on Castle Hill. He continued to support the trade union after the strike and both his solicitor's practice and newspaper suffered as a consequence. While in Cornwall in 1885 he was declared bankrupt with £9,870 liabilities. He fled to Ireland to avoid arrest. If he had not already turned to drink he was soon to do so. In 1893, while working in Grantham as a teacher, he was frequently intoxicated and was gaoled for neglecting his own children. Back in Huddersfield in 1897 he recounted his experiences at temperance meetings. He was discharged from his bankruptcy in 1899. He is best known for his novels of local life, such as 'Ben o' Bills the Luddite' and 'Sister Gertrude'.

DANIEL FREDERICK EDWARD SYKES
1856-1920 ZZZ05424 (Kirklees Cultural Services)

CHAPTER FOUR

THE TOWN THAT
BOUGHT ITSELF

THE FIRST PROPOSAL to buy the Ramsden Estate had been put to the Council in 1894 when Cllr E A Beaumont met with Baron Rothschild and secured an offer of financial assistance if the purchase was agreed. The idea was rejected as being 'one hundred years too soon'. Wilfrid Dawson, elected in 1917, revived the plan. The Council did not yet have the legal powers to purchase the estate, which would require an Act of Parliament. However, Sam Copley, a locally born millionaire and former Berry Brow hairdresser, had made his fortune in America and he offered to help. He was happy to own his native town if the Council proved unable to buy it from him.

Great secrecy surrounded the dealings. It was vital that Sir John Frechville Ramsden, the 6th Baronet, did not suspect that it was the Council behind the purchase of the estate. Considering the strained relations over the years it was feared that he would totally reject the sale, or try and squeeze as much money out of them as possible - especially since the Ramsdens were heavily burdened with debt. It seems, however, that Colonel Beadon, the Ramsden agent, was aware of what was happening, which was more than could be said for most of the councillors. Ramsden's asking price was £1,500,000. An offer was made of £1,000,000 and bargaining continued until Ramsden stuck at £1,333,000 and the Council's negotiators at £1,250,000. Then a newspaper leaked the story of the Council's involvement and Cllr Dawson was rushed

A PAGEANT FLOAT 1968 ZZZ05440 (Trevor Kipling)

'Huddersfield buys itself' is re-enacted on a float during the Borough Centenary Pageant in 1968.

into clinching the deal at the asking price, which Copley accepted on 24 October 1919.

It was now up to Dawson to inform the Council and persuade them to buy the estate from Copley, arguing that it 'would forever stamp Huddersfield as a pioneer in Municipal enterprise'. Never again would they have to go cap in hand to a landlord and the future development of the town would be in their own hands. It was even a bargain - cheaper per yard than calico. The only obstacle now was getting the Lands Bill passed to allow them to do it. There was opposition from the Lords Spiritual since the estate controlled several curates' livings, which they were reluctant to entrust to the mercies of secular or nonconformist councillors. The Bill was passed on 29 September 1930, earning Huddersfield the reputation of the 'Town that Bought itself'.

But there was still a final cliff-hanger to come in this drama. The money, borrowed from a variety of lenders in short term loans, had to be paid over by open drafts from London banks, which could be cashed by anyone who had them in their possession. The bank providing the drafts had them hand delivered to the Borough Treasurer, Ernest Dyson, in person, in his office. Worried about having charge of them for the two days before they could be paid into the seller's account, he had them sewn into special pockets in his waistcoat. He travelled down to London with escorts, but was unnerved when they insisted on a night at the theatre. However, all went well and the sale was duly completed. The estate began paying for itself in a few years

and even made a profit of £1-million, but it was not until 1972 that the debt and interest was finally paid off. Ironically, within two years Huddersfield Borough Council was abolished and not long after that, the piecemeal sale of the 'Town That Bought Itself' began.

Fact File

After the First World War, Huddersfield 'adopted' two French villages. Hermies and Havrin Court had been the scene of fierce fighting and were the location of several British cemeteries. In 1922 Huddersfield helped with the building of a waterworks and the reconstruction of houses, schools and churches.

A committee had been established in 1920 to raise money for a memorial to the 4,500-plus men from Huddersfield and district who had died in the First World War. The fund fell short of the £100,000 target but £54,000 was raised. A monument consisting of a semi-circular colonnade and a 60-feet-high central column carrying a cross was built at the top of the main walk in Greenhead Park for £14,000. The remaining £40,000 was invested to give the infirmary a return of over £2,000 a year. 'Thus the illustrious military dead have been honoured and the suffering civilians will be even better cared for.' The memorial was unveiled on Saturday 26 April 1924 by Northern Command General Sir Charles Harington in a civic ceremony described as the 'epilogue of a poignant tragedy'.

BRITISH DYES

During the Boer War, Read Holliday and Sons manufactured picric acid for the explosive Lyddite which resulted in a massive explosion at the works in 1900. The demand for both explosives and dyestuffs caused such concern to the government during the First World War that they created a new company, British Dyes, which bought Holliday's out. A vast 450-acre greenfield site at Dalton was acquired for the construction of the new works. This later became the world famous company ICI which branched out into agrichemicals and pharmaceuticals. Read Holliday's grandson, Lionel Brook Holliday, who had served on the Western Front as a major, started his own company further along Leeds Road.

GREENHEAD PARK 1957 HI51036

The war memorial in the photograph was dedicated in 1924.

The town could attempt some closure on a war that had not been popular locally. Huddersfield had had one of the highest rates of conscientious objectors in the country. The main problem facing the Borough, and the country, was the provision of the promised 'Homes fit for Heroes'. In June 1925, in what The Examiner condemned as a 'Cruel Outrage', the new war memorial was defaced by large black letters with the question, 'Why not build us some houses to live in?'

The following year, Greenhead Park was the scene of the commemoration of a different kind of struggle - the fight against the Factory System. A children's playground was dedicated to Richard Oastler, the 'Factory King', who had led the Ten Hour movement and the resistance to the New Poor Law in the 1830s.

The diamond jubilee of the incorporation of the Borough fortunately fell in 1928, after the tensions of the General Strike and miners' lockout and before the Wall Street crash. There was a mood of optimism which was expressed in the motto 'The best is yet to be'. The Huddersfield Examiner summed up the feeling of local pride: 'The sixty years of municipal activity which are now being commemorated have shown a record of advance in every sphere which cannot be bettered by any town in the UK and the most notable mark of these developments has been their practicality.'

The inauguration of several new schemes coincided with the jubilee. A new omnibus garage at Leeds Road, claimed to be the most up to date in country, was opened by mayoress. Two new turbines were installed at the St Andrews Road power station and it was hoped this would further reduce the charges for electricity. Since 1910 a destructor, or refuse incinerator, had cut costs by producing steam for the turbines, which, by 1923, were also generating power for the tram system. It saved the Borough the equivalent of 4,000 tons of coal a year. New plant was also installed at the Cooper Bridge Sewage works in 1928. Sanitation was still a prime concern of the Council, who, with an eye for detail, had pioneered the introduction of municipal metal dustbins by 1918! 90% of the rubbish

was incinerated in destructors leaving only 10% for tipping. In 1896 a new tip had been bought from the railway company near Lockwood viaduct, right at the edge of the borough (and uncomfortably close to Beaumont Park) and this was in use up to the 1920s.

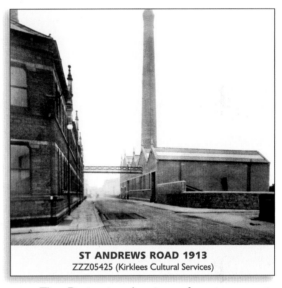

ST ANDREWS ROAD 1913
ZZZ05425 (Kirklees Cultural Services)

The Destructor, burning refuse to generate electricity.

The first sod of the Cambridge Road Baths was cut by the mayor in jubilee year. This had been proposed before the First World War, due to the popularity of the public baths at Ramsden Street. They had been built following the purchase of the Gymnasium Hall for £2,000 in 1880; formerly the Apollo Gymnasium, established in the late 1840s. Cambridge Road Baths were finally opened in August 1931, with not only the slipper and swimming baths already popular at Ramsden Street, but foam and shower baths and a café.

HUDDERSFIELD NATURALIST'S SOCIETY

Huddersfield Naturalist's Society, originating from a meeting in 1847, was reputed to be the oldest provincial society of its sort. Although composed mainly of working men, the society did have its wealthy patrons with Lord Dartmouth among their number. Huddersfield Archaeological and Topographical Association was founded in 1864 and took the lead in establishing a Yorkshire-wide association in 1871. It begun excavations at the Roman Fort at Slack in 1865 having agreed that, since it was on their land, any finds would by deposited in the Waterworks Commissioners' Spring Street offices, until a suitable museum was available. Huddersfield Literary and Scientific Society discussed the building of an 'Athenaeum' in 1866, along with HNS and HATA, and part of Alderman Denham's ambitious park plans included acquiring Greenhead Hall as a museum for use by all the local societies. One pioneering local naturalist was Samuel Eddison, (1800-1870), founder of the auctioneers' firm whose gothic-style offices with their wrought iron gates are still in High Street.

From 1934, during the winter months, the large pool was closed and converted into a dance hall. This reached a height of popularity during the Second World War but was discontinued in 1956 when new venues emerged for modern dance crazes.

Despite its progressiveness and commitment to education and intellectual improvement, there were two facilities that Huddersfield lagged behind many other towns in providing - a purpose built library and a museum.

The main champion of a town museum was Seth Lister Mosley; a painter and decorator turned naturalist, he established his own Museum near Beaumont Park in 1880. In frustration at the Council's disinterest he sold off some of his rarest specimens in 1893. He was appointed part-time curator of the collections at the Technical College, which was taken over by the Borough in 1902 and opened as a public museum on a part-time basis. In 1919, the manufacturer and antiquarian, Legh Tolson donated Ravensknowle Hall and grounds to the town in memory of two nephews killed in the war. The Hall, 'one of the best arranged and most substantial residences in Yorkshire', had been for a time the residence of chemical manufacturer, Robert Holliday. The stamp collection he had previously bequeathed to the town now returned home. At the age of 72, S L Mosley was rewarded for his lifelong dedication by being made curator. A new wing was added in 1935 for use as lecture rooms and to house the museum's growing collection of textile exhibits.

Demands for a free public library had been made at least as early as 1852, during the protests at the Ramsden heir coming of age celebrations. By 1876 there were public libraries in 76 towns but Huddersfield was not amongst them. A poll in 1881 on whether to adopt the Public Libraries Act met with

CHURCH STREET, SOMERSET BUILDINGS 2005
H151723k (Alan Brooke)

Somerset Buildings, the home of Huddersfield's first free library and art gallery.

overwhelming apathy. A 'Free Libraries Committee' campaigned throughout the 1880s, meeting the same objections as those to a museum. Councillors believed that such facilities should rely on voluntary effort, not the overburdened ratepayers. Reading and nature study were thought of as pastimes, on a par with gardening or keeping pigeons rather than cultural or educational activities. By the 1890s the trade unions were behind the free library movement and the case was

put forward in a powerful pamphlet called 'In Darkest Huddersfield' by 'Abu Ben Adhem'.

The debate intensified over how best to mark Queen Victoria's diamond jubilee. Although the advocates of a tower on Castle Hill attracted the most wealthy sponsors, it was agreed that some of the funds could be used for a library and other worthwhile causes. A library and art gallery were opened in 1898 in rooms rented at Ramsden's Somerset Buildings on Church Street. This soon outgrew the space. After the first World War a memorial library to the fallen was considered but abandoned in favour of the Greenhead Park monument. Eventually the Cloth Hall was demolished in 1930 with the intention of using the site for a library and art gallery. However, to the rage of art-lovers and bibliophiles, the Corporation leased the site to the Union Cinema Company. It remained a car park until July 1935 when work began on the Ritz Cinema, described as 'Yorkshire's most luxurious theatre'. The contractors, J Wimpenny & Co, had already built the Waterloo and other cinemas, but their greatest surviving monument is the massive Titanic Mill at Linthwaite.

The Cloth Hall was not the oldest landmark to disappear in the 1930s. The former Shears Inn, by now merely No 1 Leeds Road, was reputed to be 'the oldest house in Huddersfield'. Demolition in 1937 revealed 'fortress'-like walls and massive curved oak baulks. It had formerly stood adjacent to an equally (or more) ancient half-timbered building - probably the old Huddersfield Hall. The 1937 scheme demolished 232 houses in a maze of

THE THOMAS STREET AREA BEFORE THE SLUM CLEARANCE OF 1937 ZZZ05426 (Kirklees Cultural Services)

courts and alleys between Northumberland Street, Northgate, and Leeds Road, provoking comparison with 'a scene from the Spanish [civil] war'. Residents of Thomas Street were still complaining two years later that they had not yet been re-housed and much of the area remained like a bomb-site until the 1950s. Outside town, the construction of a massive estate was begun at Brakenhall and, by mid 1939, 700 of the planned 947 houses were completed. At Rawthorpe, roads were being laid for an estate of 960 houses.

'It can be said that Huddersfield has improved, is improving, and will improve,' announced The Examiner in 1937. High Street Buildings, begun in 1930 and designed by local architect Norman Culley, set the tone with what was grandly termed 'a modernist Renaissance treatment', rejecting any elaborate ornamentation. Stone cleaning of existing buildings became the vogue and in 1930 The Examiner (whose own offices had received the treatment) declared 'it is very probable that in no other provincial town has so much cleaning work been done within the last year or so'.

New offices and shop fronts appeared on Cloth Hall Street complementing the style of the Ritz Cinema, while the fashion for gleaming facades led to even the old White Hart pub being painted white! National chain stores such as Marks & Spencer's on New Street and Burton's in the Market Place introduced their own characteristic pilaster decorated facades. A large extension in the

Burton's gleaming white façade dominates the Market Place in this view down New Street. It is now a branch of Macdonalds.

NEW STREET c1960 H151017

plain modern style, 'making maximum use of horizontal lines', was also added to the Industrial Society [Cooperative] Building on Buxton Road in 1936. It had already been enlarged in 1903, annexing the neighbouring Victoria Hall, to make it the largest store in town. By now it was rivalled by Heywood's, which opened new premises on Market Street in January 1930, including a 'luxuriously appointed café' seating 450 and an 'electric lift to all departments'.

From April to June 1939, at a cost of £30,000, new sewers were laid along the whole length of the main thoroughfare from St George's Square to Buxton Road and the road surface asphalted. Huddersfield's first press button signals for pedestrian crossings were also installed at the New Street/Westgate crossroads and the first tall concrete lampposts appeared. Already the growing influence of the motorcar lobby, which was to have such a profound effect on future planning, was being felt. In 1935 the National Motorists' Association held what it claimed was the largest ever meeting of British motorists in the Temperance Hall. This was called to oppose the new 30mph speed limit for built-up areas, introduced by the transport minister Hoare-Belisha. Despite the local papers reporting a fatal accident almost every week, the car owners claimed there was no need for a limit which made every driver into a 'potential criminal' and which encouraged the police to use 'Bolshevik methods'.

NEW STREET 1939 ZZZ05427 (Kirklees Cultural Services)

'Take Courage'. Soon the new building was swathed in sandbags and a first-aid post and an emergency ward took the place of the proposed Children's Library and Art Gallery.

Huddersfield escaped the Second World War almost unscathed. This is somewhat surprising since it was home to ICI, one of the countries largest chemical works, (successor

Another potential library site was released by the closure of the Ramsden Street Chapel in 1933, which was bought by the council and demolished in 1936 along with the adjacent late-1830s 'Guild Hall', once owned by Joseph Kaye. The controversial plans for the new library were revealed in December 1937. Approval of the library's sculptures by James Woodford, who had worked on decorations for the Queen Mary and studied at the British School in Rome, scraped through by a single vote the following year, one Councillor describing the friezes as 'grotesque'. Even today some people think the building more evocative of 1930s Nuremburg than of Huddersfield. The library was officially opened on 15 April 1940 and appropriately the first book taken out was Phyllis Bentley's

THE LIBRARY c1960 HI51013

to British Dyes, which had taken over Read Holliday & Sons in 1915) and several vital engineering works. The first bombs fell on 29 August 1940 in a field at Hall Bower below Castle Hill. In a raid the following year some damage was done to Wellington Mill, Lindley. But Huddersfield's worst-ever tragedy was not the result of enemy action. On 31 October 1941 49 people were killed, mostly women and girls, when Booth's clothing works on John William Street burnt down. Formerly an elegant warehouse of the 1890s, it had inappropriately been converted to a factory with inadequate fire escapes.

THE LIBRARY 2005 H151724k (Alan Brooke)

This photograph shows a detail of the sculptured friezes.

The post-war years brought nationalisation and the end of municipal control of energy supplies, although electricity continued to be generated on the St Andrews Road site into the 1970s. It also saw the resumption of a massive programme of slum clearance and new housing. One of Huddersfield's most ambitious post-war schemes was the demolition of the rows of terraces along Rashcliffe Hill which, by 1958, had been replaced with flats. Around 4,000 new houses had been completed throughout the Borough by the beginning of the 1960s. However, Huddersfield's earliest council houses were among the last to go. The area between St Andrews Road and Turnbridge was not cleared until the late 1970s - to be replaced by a vast car park.

The 1960s and early 70s brought Huddersfield's great leap forward into modernity - or, to some, unforgivable acts of short-sighted municipal vandalism, achieving what the Luftwaffe had failed to do. Plans for the ring road were published in 1959, necessitating the demolition of a great swathe of buildings around the town. Symbolic of the break with the past was the loss of the old Textile Department of the College of Technology. Opened by Asquith in 1920, the converted rug mill had been presented to the Corporation by local industry. Some town streets were also widened for traffic, involving the loss of the Elite Fish & Chip Café at the top of High Street, where one rear window pane still had scratched upon it, 'Miss Robinson 1765'.

In the 1960s all the buildings between Buxton Road and Corporation Street, including the Woolpack (Joseph Kaye's former pub), and the 'Penny Savings Bank', were demolished for the 'Murrayfield development' of flat-roofed shops and a high-rise office block, 'Ramsden House'. The only relief to their

NEW STREET 1957 HI51010

austerity is a colourful mosaic mural that depicts the history of the woollen industry. It was designed by local artist Harold Blackburn and made under his supervision in Venice.

The second phase of development saw the demolition of properties between Peel Street and Queen Street. Many of these were owned by the Corporation: the police and fire stations and the clinic, the latter well remembered by those who, as children, had teeth more or less brutally extracted. This became the site of the Queensgate Market. Its massive ceramic

The Prudential Insurance building, seen in the foreground to the right, was designed by A Waterhouse, the architect of Manchester Town Hall. It is unusual for the town in that it is built of brick and terra-cotta tiles. On the left hand side of the street the copper dome of Hughes' Huddersfield Banking Co building can be seen.

NEW STREET, NOW PEDESTRIANISED 2005 H151725k (Alan Brooke)

Fact File

Established in 1827, the Huddersfield Banking Company was only the second joint stock bank in the country, created under an Act to prevent a recurrence of the banking crisis of the previous year. In 1837 Charles William Sikes, (the son of failed banker Shakespeare Garrick Sikes), became a cashier for the company. Concerned with the problems of the poor, he invented the idea of Penny Savings Banks and many were formed at Mechanics' Institutes and mills after 1850. He also initiated the Post Office Savings Bank scheme which, backed by Rowland Hill of 'Penny Post' fame, won government support in 1861. In 1937 it was proposed to mark his residence at 48 Spring Street with a plaque.

A PORTRAIT OF CHARLES W SIKES
ZZZ05428 (Kirklees Cultural Services)

A view of the ceramic panels by artist Fritz Steller.

QUEENSGATE MARKET HALL 1969 ZZZ05429 (Trevor Kipling)

sculptured panels overlooking the ring road, far from adding the intended 'colour and interest', only emphasise the building's crudity and oppressiveness.

In 1970 the beautiful ornate market hall, once the pride of the town, was demolished to be replaced by an unimaginative block of flat-roofed shops of concrete and glass. A massive blank 'Berlin Wall' now dominates the area where once stood the elegant Georgian buildings of Queen Street. Much of Ramsden Street, including the Theatre Royal and the popular baths (where 1960 Olympic champion Anita Lonsbrough trained), disappeared under the pretentiously named 'Piazza'. But one of the saddest losses was the Pack Horse Hotel and its yard, one of the town's oldest and most popular pubs, which, despite a fierce campaign, was eventually demolished to make way for a characterless

shopping mall opened in 1971.

But it was not only ugly, uninspired commercial buildings which blemished the town. Between October 1965 and June 1977 a new Civic Centre, with adjacent Police Station and Magistrates' Court, replaced the municipal buildings lost in the Ramsden Street clearance. This entailed the demolition of a swathe of old property between High Street and Manchester Street, including the notorious Water Lane (already considered a slum 'black spot' in 1930), the intriguingly named Glass Alley and the former Mr Love's pawnshop. The slum clearance was welcome, but the buildings that arose were hardly designed to instil a sense of civic pride. The 1960s also saw the erection of several unsightly tower blocks skirting the ring road at Southgate, accommodating government offices (the former telephone exchange and

THE SHAMBLES c1970 ZZZ05430 (Trevor Kipling)

The popular shopping street which runs alongside the old Market Hall.

THE SHAMBLES c1970 ZZZ05431 (Trevor Kipling)

The photograph shows a stall shortly before the demolition of the old Market Hall. Note the greengrocer's sign, 'See you all in the new market hall'.

Inland Revenue), and council flats.

Ironically, while this destruction was being planned, or actually underway, pride in Huddersfield's heritage, and some nostalgia for what was being lost, was expressed by the 1968 commemoration of the Centenary of Huddersfield's Incorporation. On the suggestion of the local government workers' union NALGO (now Unison), a Civic Exhibition representing each department of the Council was held in the Town Hall, attracting 40,000 people. In addition, a pageant with floats depicted scenes from the town's history, such as the Incorporation and the buying of the Ramsden Estate. The same year also saw the journey of the last of the much-loved trolleybuses, which had replaced Huddersfield's pioneering tram system in the 1930s.

Six years later the Borough of Huddersfield itself became history, absorbed by the amalgamation with neighbouring Urban District Councils and Dewsbury Borough to form Kirklees Metropolitan Council. The merger was so unpopular that the name eventually agreed was taken from a location actually outside of the new authority's boundaries - the Kirklees Estate of the Armytage family and famed burial place of bold Robin Hood. Needless to say, there were those who suspected that the new authority was Robin Hood in reverse!

The last mayor of Huddersfield was sworn in on 22 May 1973. The unveiling of the new Sports Centre by Princess Anne in July and opening of the Ring Road in November of that year were among the Council's final acts. A new bus station was opened in Upperhead

The Lockwood Band joining the Borough Centenary pageant.

HIGH STREET 1968 ZZZ05432 (Trevor Kipling)

WESTGATE 1968 ZZZ05433 (Trevor Kipling)

Huddersfield's last trolleybus on its farewell journey.

THE PARISH CHURCH c1955 HI51014

This view of the church incorporates part of the tracery of trolleybus wires which were such a feature of the town and its environs.

Row in 1974, although not yet completed. As councillors rushed to empty the civic purse before the new super-authority got hold of it, £15,000 was spent on a 'Venetian fountain' for St George's Square. Mercifully, it only worked for a couple of years before Huddersfield's weather damaged the soft limestone and the fountain had to be removed. It now serves as the world's most expensive Christmas tree stand. On 27 March 1974 Huddersfield Council held its last meeting. After 106 years the independent Borough of Huddersfield went out with the bangs of a fireworks display in Greenhead Park.

The 1980s and 1990s were to witness new problems as central government policies led to the unravelling of many of Huddersfield's municipal achievements, especially the selling-off of council houses and the de-regulation of buses. Budgetary constraints and the rule of the internal market led to the reduction of direct council control over services and the disposal of assets that even included ground rents. Gradually, the 'Town that Bought Itself' became a town that was selling itself.

These decades saw the swansong of the basic industry on which the town had been founded and with it the greatest transformation of the local urban landscape in over a century. The roots of this decline can be traced to the end of the 19th century when Britain's position as workshop of the world began to be challenged.

In 1892 Henry Lister & Sons, silk plush and worsted manufacturer of Ashbrow Mills, were blaming the USA's McKinley tariff for the 'considerable losses' leading to their

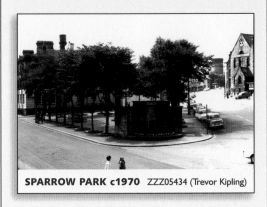

SPARROW PARK c1970 ZZZ05434 (Trevor Kipling)

bankruptcy. The plan was to circumvent the tariff by opening a spinning plant in Jamestown, New York, equipped with machinery from England. Another approach was to increase productivity and, with this in mind, Messrs Learoyd & Co built a new factory in 1896 on a revolutionary principle. Trafalgar Mill, with its stately frontage onto Leeds Road, was designed to operate on a single level to increase efficiency. Yarn came in at one entrance and passed through each stage of the manufacturing process around the mill to emerge at the other as finished cloth. When Technical College textile students visited in 1899 they were struck by the 'exceptional orderliness and neatness' of the mill. Other firms responded by introducing faster looms, replacing male by female labour and two-loom working; none of which proved popular with the weavers.

One employer tried less confrontational methods to get better results from his workforce. George Thomson of Woodhouse Mill, Deighton, was a staunch believer in cooperation and corresponded with John Ruskin and William Morris. In 1886 he introduced a profit sharing scheme but confessed in 1891 that in recent years there had not been much profit to distribute due to high wool prices. Around 3d per £1 of wages were given in shares and 80% of the workers were shareholders. By 1908 the mill was being run by a committee and provided an 8-hour day, a pension scheme, a sick fund, a marriage portion and full lay-off pay. No married women, or non-union labour was employed. In 1912 when Thomson was made mayor the 'co-partnership' scheme was still going strong.

One of the main technological innovations introduced in the 20th century was electrically driven machinery. Kaye & Stewart, fancy manufacturers of Broadfield Mill, were one of the first firms to embrace and implement the concept. By 1919 they were using a three cylinder compound engine and generator delivering 625 kilovolt amps with each group of 20 looms being driven by a motor. One pioneer of this new technology was Ernest Brook, who began manufacturing electric motors with eight workers at Threadneedle Street in 1903, moving to Nelson Mill on Colne Road in 1905 and then to a purpose built factory on St Thomas's Road in 1915. Brook Motors was fast becoming one of the leaders in the field.

MANCHESTER ROAD 1982 ZZZ05435 (Brooke Collection)

The photograph shows fire engines attending a relatively minor fire in part of Springdale Mill. Last occupied by Harold Haigh, the building has now been demolished.

While those firms weaving khaki thrived, the post-war depression and the gold standard crisis quelled any optimism. Employers tried to slash costs by wage cutting, leading to some 20,000 textile workers striking for several months in 1925 and in 1930. However, it was generally agreed that Huddersfield was not so badly affected as other areas, mainly due to the diversity of its industry. The textile trade itself was not reliant on a narrow market because of the variety of its products. Despite foreign competition, the credit squeeze and the long disputes, unemployment in the town was relatively low at approximately 5,000 even in 1930. By 1935 it had fallen to 3,653, the lowest for eight years, and there was even a shortage of textile workers. Some mills were working overtime in response to improvements in the export trade and firms looked to recruit from 'the distressed areas'. Engineering firms like Brook Motors, the Prospect Ironworks and David Brown & Sons were also making extensions to their works. Nevertheless, there was some shock when the old firm of Vickerman's, which traced its ancestry to the 18th century, closed down in 1938 and Taylor Hill Mill was taken over by the Czech firm Bruck & Englesmann. The loss of hundreds of jobs with the closure of the massive United Thread cotton works at Meltham Mills and of the Slaithwaite Spinning Co brought the depression uncomfortably close to the town, but by now, with war looming, military contracts were already helping to revive the local economy.

The post-war, post-colonial world saw Britain's dominance further reduced. By 1958 cheap Italian and Japanese textiles were being dumped on the market and countries like Canada and the US had placed a tariff on British cloth. Import restrictions, excessive duties and unfair competition were being blamed for the gloomy prospects in 1967. To complaints that Huddersfield's fine worsteds were in fact pricing themselves out of the market, producers replied '… with increasing taxation, social benefits, insurance, high interest rates and increases in almost every item of expense, there is little that manufacturers can do…'. Some blamed the slowness of firms in meeting the challenge, by not investing in new machinery or responding to new fashions.

The 1970s saw the closure of mills and the disappearance of old firms as take-overs by conglomerates such as Allied Textiles or Illingworth Morris led to 'rationalisation'. By 1980 the industry was facing its worse depression since the 1930s. During this decade and the 1990s the decline accelerated with the loss of thousands of jobs and the transformation of the physical appearance of the town as, one after another, familiar mills and their landmark chimneys disappeared.

In 1980 Trafalgar Mill, by now part of the Illingworth Morris combine, ceased production in what The Examiner dubbed a 'Sign of the times … an empty mill'. The once model textile factory was leased for industrial units by a new owner in 1982. Fortunately its adaptability to such a use saved it from demolition. It also survived

a fire in the central office block occupied by a computer firm in 1994. The fate of Zetland Mill on Queen Street South was more typical. Having lain empty for two years it was badly damaged by fire in 1980 and had to be demolished. Within half a mile of it others were razed to the ground over the following three or four years, including the tall Phoenix Mill at Rashcliffe which had

WESTGATE, A DEMONSTRATION 1982
H151726k (Alan Brooke)

A demonstration against factory closures and job losses. The Ramsden Estate building on Railway Street can be seen in the background.

been empty for some time, Engine Bridge Mill at Folly Hall, the mills of Colne Road, including Britannia Mill, and those along Albert Street at Lockwood such as Broadfield Mill. The biggest complex to disappear was the former Starkey's Factory at Springdale Mills, Longroyd Bridge, once the biggest woollen factory in the town. Starkey's had been wound-up in 1907 but the mills, under multiple tenants, survived almost intact until the whole site was cleared in the early 1980s, eventually making way for a DIY store.

ZETLAND MILL, QUEEN STREET SOUTH, DURING DEMOLITION 1981 ZZZ05436 (Brooke Collection)

CHAPEL HILL c1980 ZZZ05437 (Brooke Collection)

The demolition of the former Engine Bridge Mill has just begun. This mill can be seen in L S Lowry's painting of Huddersfield, purchased by the Council in 1965.

There continued to be some glimmers of optimism. Larchfield Mill, closed in 1979, was reopened in 1981 by Fred Lawton & Son as part of the expansion of their neighbouring Firth Street Mill. However, the firm moved to Meltham Mills in 1988 (following the closure of Case Tractors on that site), and the Firth Street premises were again empty. Luckily the proximity to the University across the canal made them ideal for renovation and, with imagination and a great deal of investment, they were reborn as lecture rooms - a fate the founder of Larchfield Mill, George Brook Junior, and his naturalist son George who lectured on embryology at Edinburgh University, would no doubt have approved.

In 1979 Folly Hall Mills were modernised at a cost of £750,000 but by 1982 had closed down. Joseph Lumb & Sons, yarn spinners, bought the mills from the executors of Joseph Kaye, the builder, in the 1870s. 'Jesse' Lumb's were employing over 1,000 people in the 1930s and were so short of labour after the war that women workers were bussed in from the Barnsley area. The business was later taken over by Allied Textiles whose chairman was J E Lumb. Described by G S Phillips in the 1840s 'as so many Aladdin's palaces', much of the mill complex was demolished in 1994, most of it reduced to a bingo hall car park. Only two buildings remain on the site; one of them, overlooking the river, is the mill rebuilt by Kaye after the 1844 fire. Despite proposals to convert it into flats, the undoubtedly most elegant mill building in Huddersfield is slowly succumbing to the weather. Pigeons flock in and out of its smashed windows, its very neglect an invitation to vandals and arsonists. It is now on the 'buildings at risk register'.

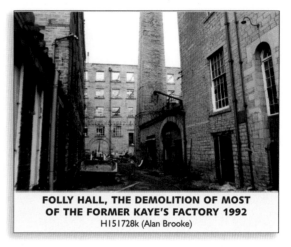

FOLLY HALL, THE DEMOLITION OF MOST OF THE FORMER KAYE'S FACTORY 1992
H151728k (Alan Brooke)

FIRTH STREET, CANALSIDE MILLS 2005
H151727k (Alan Brooke)

The Canalside Mills are now part of the University.

Although Folly Hall is a listed building this is no guarantee of its future, as shown by the fate of Kings Mill. Despite its historical association with the site of the former Almondbury manorial corn mill and the listing of the 1840s part of the structure, Kirklees Council, at a public inquiry in 1984, backed the building contractor who lobbied for its demolition. This was opposed by the Victorian Society and Save Britain's Heritage, but, strangely, not by Huddersfield Civic Society. The Department of the Environment refused consent for demolition, but no alternative use was found for the mill. On 5 June 1992, while other buildings were being cleared on the site, it was gutted by fire. Three weeks later, in what is apparently a common hazard facing empty listed buildings, another fire destroyed the remaining timbers. The mill was totally demolished and replaced by flats.

The feasibility of adapting mill buildings for other uses was ably demonstrated in 1984 by the proposal to convert Albion Mills into flats. The developers foresaw that urban living would become more popular as industry deserted the town. This was proved by the conversion of Priestroyd Mill and ironworks in 2004 to provide not only luxury flats but also a restaurant and leisure facilities. With the property boom mill conversions have also caught on in the surrounding villages and many of those who rushed to demolish mills in the previous two decades must now be kicking themselves. The fact remains that there is a reluctance to conserve industrial heritage for its own sake if there is no financial incentive.

Other locally grown industries have also closed down or announced they are to sever their long connection with the area, including the chemical firm of L B Holliday, Brook Motors and Hopkinson's Gears. However, the textile industry is not entirely dead. Despite losses in 1980, the firm of John L Brierley Ltd bounced back to celebrate its centenary in 1993. It still continues rayon spinning at Turnbridge Mills, part of which dates back to 1846 - probably making it the oldest textile mill in the country still being used for the purpose it was intended.

Although vestiges of the textile and other industries remain, the way of life and the rich culture they sustained are gone forever. It was often a hard life, which took its toll in accidents and disease, but there is no doubt that the loss of the sense of community, and the pride people felt in their work, has left a huge void. Creating a meaningful way of filling that void is one of the greatest challenges of the 21st century.

Fact File

TURNBRIDGE MILL WITH THE CANAL BRIDGE IN OPERATION 2005 H151729k (Alan Brooke)

The original 'Turnbridge' became a lift bridge and the present structure bears the date 1865. On the River Colne, 'Engine Bridge' was named in the 18th century after a waterwheel driven pumping engine which raised water through wooden pipes to a reservoir at Upperhead Row. On one occasion a trout was blamed for blocking the pipes. Industrial pollution in the early 19th century sealed the fate of both the water supply and the trout.

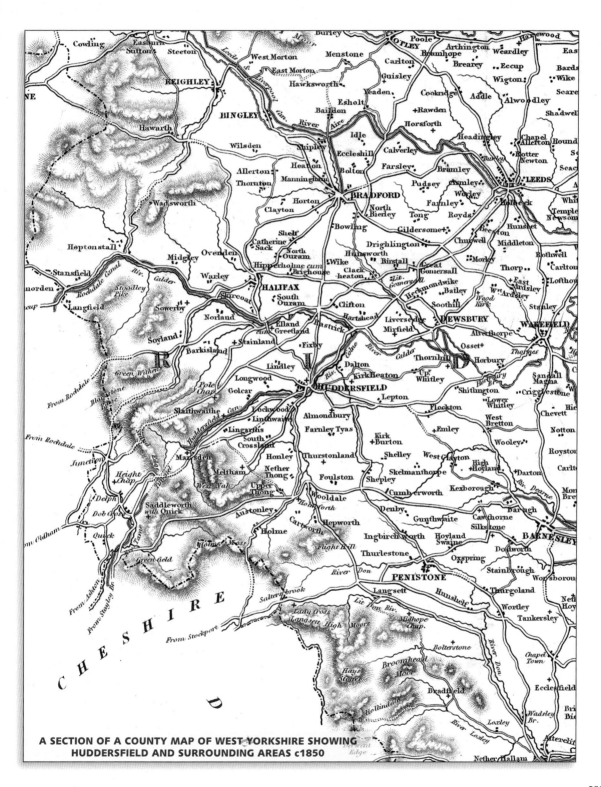

**A SECTION OF A COUNTY MAP OF WEST YORKSHIRE SHOWING
HUDDERSFIELD AND SURROUNDING AREAS c1850**

CHAPTER FIVE

GOD HELPS THEM WHO HELP THEMSELVES

LESSONS HAVE BEEN learned from the mistakes of the 1960s and early 1970s. New developments now offer far more exciting possibilities, while better efforts at public consultation defuse some of the controversy and anger. The Kingsgate shopping centre, despite taking years to come to fruition largely due to wrangling between rival developers, created not only a covered mall, housing national and independent retailers, but successfully incorporated existing buildings into the scheme. Although some attractive old buildings were lost, including listed ones, the remaining old shops in King Street and their associated yards were refurbished sympathetically, retaining much of their character and creating a pleasant environment for shoppers, or diners at the many cafés and restaurants.

The future of the controversial Queensgate Market site, the piazza and the library are all under discussion as the Council has ambitions to redevelop the area to rival Kingsgate. One idea floated even involves flats or a hotel. However these plans are on hold while the future of the Queensgate Market is considered. The heated controversy continues between those who consider it ugly, claustrophobic and

THE OPEN MARKET

THE OPEN MARKET 2005 H151731k (Alan Brooke)

THE OPEN MARKET 2005 H151730k (Alan Brooke)

Huddersfield's Open Market, once the popular 'Monday Market', has been given a new lease of life by its relocation to the renovated former Wholesale Market, a listed building of 1889 designed by the Borough Surveyor R S Dugdale. Its canopy was made of prefabricated iron sections by a company in Darlington. Dugdale also designed the tram depot on Great Northern Street and the new 'Renaissance style' Police Station on Peel Street, opened in 1898.

only worthy of demolition, and those who see a local architectural gem worthy of preservation. The library too, although a familiar landmark and more popular than the market, is considered at best plain and at the worst ugly and unsuitable for its present purpose. A vocal minority has now claimed success in securing the future of these buildings by obtaining listed building status. As part of Kirklees Council's 'Renaissance Programme', plans have also been unveiled to revamp the town's gem, St George's Square, and make it more pedestrian friendly.

WORMALD'S YARD 2005 H151733k (Alan Brooke)

This is one part of old Huddersfield that has been embraced by the Kingsgate development.

KINGSGATE 2005 H151732k (Alan Brooke)

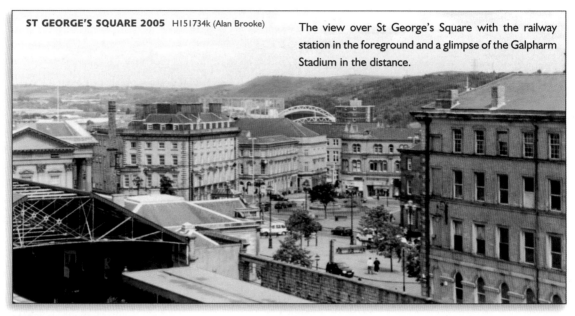

ST GEORGE'S SQUARE 2005 H151734k (Alan Brooke)

The view over St George's Square with the railway station in the foreground and a glimpse of the Galpharm Stadium in the distance.

THE MARKET PLACE c1875 ZZZ05438 (Kirklees Cultural Services)

The Market Place as it looks today after its makeover in 1998. It is now more user friendly - except for the loss of the public conveniences!

THE MARKET PLACE 2005 H151735k (Alan Brooke)

There are also plans to demolish the council flats at Rashcliffe and Southgate and, although the latter in particular are notorious eyesores, there is concern that this will lead to a further reduction of housing stock. A private developer has drawn up proposals to transform a triangle of underused industrial premises between Chapel Hill and Manchester Road into a bright, waterside development with apartments, leisure facilities and even some industry. (This is a development format that has been particularly successful in Leeds.) The narrow canal which runs through this area, regarded as 'a unique waterway', has itself been restored and was reopened as part of the millennium celebrations. Enhancing some of the less attractive areas of Huddersfield, it does provide a boon to villages in the Colne Valley which are increasingly reliant on tourism. Despite opposition and the enormous cost it has proved a worthwhile venture. The older Broad Canal has also been restored, converting another neglected industrial relic into a liquid asset for the future.

The future of Huddersfield's most famous monument, Castle Hill, is also the focus of a fierce public debate in the wake of the demolition of the pub, which had been on the site since 1852. After bitter controversy, its partially built replacement was deemed to be in breach of planning permission and was ordered to be pulled down. Opinion is divided between the options of another pub, a visitor centre of some sort or leaving the site undisturbed in deference to its archaeological importance.

CROSS CHURCH STREET c1960 HI51021

Castle Hill is just visible in the distance, showing how it makes its presence felt in the town.

The University, which can trace its genealogy back to the Technical School on the same site, has grown into a large campus and injected life into the town. Not only does it attract large numbers of British and foreign students but has regenerated the Canalside Mills, now converted into lecture rooms. Student residences, in a style reminiscent of mill architecture, have been built on brown-field sites along the river nearby. With local-born actor Patrick Stewart at the helm as chancellor, aka Captain Jean Luc Picard of the Starship Enterprise, it seems set to boldly go into the future.

Huddersfield continues to be a place of innovation. The now world-famous Media Centre provides facilities, support and encouragement for creative industries

partly in tandem with the University. As a result of its success, a £3-million expansion programme is planned to attract larger businesses and to ensure that established ones are not forced to leave the town due to lack of space needed for growth. TV and video productions, computer graphics and website design are among the skills the Centre hopes to encourage.

Known for its sporting achievements and as the birthplace of Rugby League, Huddersfield now has a state of the art all-inclusive stadium. The Galpharm Stadium (formerly MacAlpine), with its prominent 'Banana Arches', has already become a familiar landmark. Built on a former industrial site off Leeds Road, it provides not only a sports complex with swimming, golf and gym facilities but is also renowned as a conference centre and venue for pop concerts attracting such celebrities as Elton John. However there is still some nostalgia among older fans for the loss of the more innocent days of football and the old Leeds Road football stadium, designed by Archibald Leitch before the First World War, with its later 'Cowshed' stand. Adjacent to the stadium is a multi-screen cinema, now the only picture house in town - in marked contrast to when the Ritz was built in the heyday of the 'talkies', and there were well over a dozen others.

The ability of Huddersfield people to enjoy culture has often received a knocking, not least from playwright George Bernard Shaw. While visiting the town in 1909, he was recorded as saying that 'If he had £20,000 and wanted to have a very jolly time he did not think he would come to Huddersfield … it did not appear to be a place of very delirious pleasure and gaiety'. When one of his plays received a poor reception in 1930, it still seemed to him 'in a dark and pagan condition'! The last owner of the Theatre Royal seemed to agree, declaring that 'Huddersfield does not deserve a theatre'. Such cynicism has been answered by the success of the Lawrence Batley Theatre, (named after the local millionaire inventor of 'Cash and Carry'), established in the former Queen Street Methodist Chapel. Some of the Wesleyans may be turning in their graves at the 'pleasure and gaiety' brought by the drama and musical events now staged, but it has opened up many opportunities for local talent which even Shaw would have appreciated.

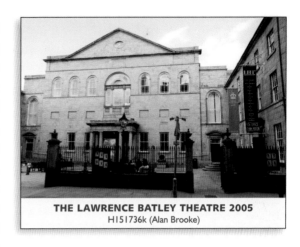

THE LAWRENCE BATLEY THEATRE 2005
H151736k (Alan Brooke)

The internationally recognised Huddersfield Choral Society is still going strong. At the festival marking the opening of the Town Hall in 1881, Sir Charles Hallé described the choir as one of the best he had ever conducted. It celebrated its centenary in 1936 with a work commissioned by Ralph Vaughan Williams, 'Dona Nobis Pacem', ('Give Us Peace') - a fitting anthem for the turbulent 30s. Sir Malcolm Sargent conducted the choir from 1932 to 1967 and was made an honorary freeman of the Borough in 1961 in recognition of his work and the contribution of the Choral Society to the town. The Society was awarded a Golden Disc on its 150th anniversary when sales of its 'Hymns Album' topped 100,000 copies. It has come a long way since when, as a narrow chapel-dominated organisation in the 1840s, its rules banned anyone who attended socialist events! Mrs Sunderland, the 'Yorkshire Queen of Song' who performed before Queen Victoria, is also commemorated by an annual competition and Lady Babirolli was amongst the judges at the centenary event. A Contemporary Music

Festival is now held annually in November that attracts leading performers and serves to emphasise that music is a living part of Huddersfield's culture.

Huddersfield's rich culture has been vitalised by successive waves of immigrants. The first recorded Irish arrived at the end of the 18th century and the building of St Patrick's Church in 1832 reflected their growing presence in the town. As a result of the commercial links established by the woollen and fancy trade there was also a small colony of German merchants who played a prominent role in the life of the town. The most famous of this group was Frederick Schwann, one of the founders of the Mechanics' Institute. The first well-known black person in the town was George Brown, manager of John Kaye & Sons, Kings Mill. An American, he was a friend of singer Paul Robeson who visited in 1939 and entertained the mill girls with a rendition of 'Ol' Man River'. By the end of the Second World War there was at least one student from Sierra Leone studying mechanical engineering at the College of Technology and one from Iraq in the textile department. 25 nationalities were represented there in 1958. Today's 'Tech' and the University continue to be proud of the number of overseas students they attract.

Following the war a large number of Poles, Ukrainians, Latvians and other East European ex-servicemen and refugees found themselves unable to return to their Stalinist dominated countries and settled in the town, finding employment in most of the major industries. The post-war labour

THE CATHOLIC CHURCH c1960 H151033

Another of the churches built by Joseph Kaye, 'a beautiful gothic structure, built entirely of fine white stone' (Leeds Mercury), it was dedicated to St Patrick in 1833.

shortage, particularly in textiles, led to the encouragement of workers from the West Indies and the Indian sub-continent. By 1959 there was a Huddersfield Muslim Educational and Cultural Society, which worked with the Cooperative Education Department to deliver English classes for Pakistanis in the Fraternity Hall. An International Liaison Committee, backed by councillors, was set up in the 1960s to assist people settling in the town. It was based at Spring Grove School which, built as a model school, has always proved innovatory. Huddersfield gave sanctuary to Belgian refugees in the First World War, to Basque children in the 1930s and since 1999 has received asylum seekers from over 54 countries. The town now has viable Kurdish and Ethiopian communities. St Patrick's Day, the Asian Melah and the Caribbean Carnival have become highlights of the cultural calendar and seem likely to remain so as long as they retain the support of their communities. The golden

domes of the Sikh temple have even added an exotic tinge to Huddersfield's otherwise unremarkable skyline.

Perhaps due to their deep-rooted egalitarianism, Huddersfield people have never really gone in for monumental statues (apart from war memorials). King Edward VII, whose statue stands on what was the old Infirmary forecourt, is the only royal on display. However, Huddersfield born Prime Minister Harold Wilson now strides confidently forward outside the railway station. It is a monument to a local lad made good, rather than a political leader, although he was driven by the same concerns that motivated Joshua Hobson and the founders of the Borough. Speaking before the 1964 election he declared his commitment to improving conditions in towns like Huddersfield, where a third of homes still didn't have a bathroom and a quarter had no piped hot water.

Huddersfield has long been the butt of music hall jokes about ferrets, flat caps and flatter vowels. And there may even be some truth in the stereotype of its people as being dour, gritty and thrifty. But there is no denying the achievements of the townsfolk over the last two centuries. The motto on the coat of arms of the Huddersfield Borough, 'Juvat Impigros Deus', is often translated loosely as 'God Helps Them Who Help Themselves'. This cynical rendering still reflects some truth, for throughout the town's history 'self help' also implied collective responsibility. The ideals of hard work and 'addling brass', [earning money], have been admired but without

Fact File

A J Mundella MP opened Spring Grove School on 1 December 1880. It replaced the former 'British School' on Outcote Bank. Designed on 'the classroom system' by Edward Hughes, architect of the Market Hall, and based on the Saltaire Board School, it had 14 classrooms arranged around a central hall, with a large gallery at one end. Capable of accommodating 308 boys, 308 girls and 467 infants, it was Huddersfield's largest.

HAROLD WILSON'S STATUE

Lady Wilson and Tony Blair MP unveiled the bronze statue of Lord Harold Wilson on 9 July 1999. (She then went on to name a ballroom at the George Hotel, 'The Harold Wilson Suite'). A statue of Sir Robert Peel formerly on the site was condemned to a Council rubble heap in 1949, its soft Sicilian Marble eaten by 74 years of industrial Huddersfield's acid rain. How long Harold remains will depend more on the capriciousness of planners than the climate. Unlike Peel, he is not elevated on a lofty pedestal in a classical pose and surrounded by railings, but is accessible as befits a man of the people. The low plinth, inscribed with some of his achievements, even forms a convenient platform for the dying art of public speaking - something he would have appreciated.

HAROLD WILSON'S STATUE 2005 H151737k (Alan Brooke)

HAROLD WILSON'S STATUE 2005 H151738k (Alan Brooke)

THE VIEW OVER THE TOWN TOWARDS KILNER BANK 2005 H151739k (Alan Brooke)

Huddersfield still enjoys a rural setting.

condoning grasping, selfish individualism. Wealth was not only for the enjoyment of those who owned it, but also for improving the public good. Concern for the people's spiritual and intellectual well-being led to the building of churches, chapels, schools and Mechanics' Institutes. The infirmary, sanatoria, baths and decent housing were provided for their material welfare. These ideals were embodied in the vitality of the local Co-operative movement, Friendly Societies, Trade Unions and 'Municipal Socialism', and in the genuine concern of paternalistic employers for their workers. In a world where 'helping yourself' often has very different connotations, the values which built Huddersfield, as much as the builders and the buildings themselves, surely deserve remembrance and celebration.

ACKNOWLEDGEMENTS

We would like to thank the staff of Huddersfield Public Library, Local History and Reference departments for their help and patience. Although this book includes a lot of the authors' original research we are indebted to various local historians, past and present, who have laboured to uncover the development of various aspects of the town. The bibliography contains just some of their works. We have also relied extensively on the following newspapers: The Huddersfield Examiner, The Huddersfield Chronicle, The Huddersfield Weekly News, The Leeds Mercury, The Leeds Times, The Worker and The Yorkshire Factory Times.

BIBLIOGRAPHY

Balmforth, Owen, 'Jubilee History of the Corporation of Huddersfield' 1868-1918 *(Huddersfield 1918)*

Brook, Roy, 'The Story of Huddersfield' *(1968)*

Brook, Roy, 'The Tramways of Huddersfield' *(Advertiser Press, 1959)*

Brooke, A J and Kipling, L, 'Liberty or Death - Radicals, Republicans and Luddites 1793-1824' *(Workers History Publications, 1994)*

Bryson, Rebecca Jane, 'Working Class Living Standards in the West Yorkshire Town of Huddersfield 1870-1914', PhD Thesis *(University of Huddersfield, 1996)*

Chadwick, Stanley, 'A Bold and Faithful Journalist - Joshua Hobson 1810-1876' *(Kirklees Libraries and Museum Service, 1976)*

Crump and Ghorbal, 'A History of the Huddersfield Woollen Industry' *(Tolson Memorial Museum 1935)*

Eagles, J B, 'John Benson Pritchett - First Medical Officer of Health for Huddersfield' *(Huddersfield Local History Workshop, 1984)*

Haigh, Hilary, (Ed) 'Huddersfield - A Most Handsome Town' *(Kirklees Cultural Services, 1992)*

Law, Edward, 'Joseph Kaye - Builder of Huddersfield', *(Huddersfield Local History Society pamphlet)*

Law, Edward, 'The George Hotel' *(Internet 2004)*

Law, Edward, 'W H Crossland, Architect 1835-1908' *(ibid)*

Pearce, Cyril, 'Communistic Huddersfield', Old West Riding Vol 1, No 1, *(1981)*

Redmonds, George, 'Old Huddersfield 1500-1800' *(G R Books 1981)*

Redmonds, George, 'Almondbury Places and Place Names' *(G R Books, 1983)*

Royle, Edward, 'Queen Street Chapel and Mission' *(Huddersfield Local History Society pamphlet)*

Sykes, Arthur W, 'Ramsden Street Chapel 1825-1925' *(Advertiser Press 1925)*

Sykes, D F E, 'Huddersfield and Its Vicinity' *(Advertiser Press, 1898)*

Francis Frith
Pioneer Victorian Photographer

Francis Frith, founder of the world-famous photographic archive, was a complex and multi-talented man. A devout Quaker and a highly successful Victorian businessman, he was philosophical by nature and pioneering in outlook. By 1855 he had already established a wholesale grocery business in Liverpool, and sold it for the astonishing sum of £200,000, which is the equivalent today of over £15,000,000. Now in his thirties, and captivated by the new science of photography, Frith set out on a series of pioneering journeys up the Nile and to the Near East.

He was the first photographer to venture beyond the sixth cataract of the Nile. Africa was still the mysterious 'Dark Continent', and Stanley and Livingstone's historic meeting was a decade into the future. The conditions for picture taking confound belief. He laboured for hours in his wicker dark-room in the sweltering heat of the desert, while the volatile chemicals fizzed dangerously in their trays. Back in London he exhibited his photographs and was 'rapturously cheered' by members of the Royal Society. His reputation as a photographer was made overnight.

By the 1870s the railways had threaded their way across the country, and Bank Holidays and half-day Saturdays had been made obligatory by Act of Parliament. All of a sudden the working man and his family were able to enjoy days out, take holidays, and see a little more of the world.

With typical business acumen, Francis Frith foresaw that these new tourists would enjoy having souvenirs to commemorate their days out. For the next thirty years he travelled the country by train and by pony and trap, producing fine photographs of seaside resorts and beauty spots that were keenly bought by millions of Victorians. These prints were painstakingly pasted into family albums and pored over during the dark nights of winter, rekindling precious memories of summer excursions. Frith's studio was soon supplying retail shops all over the country, and by 1890 F Frith & Co had become the greatest specialist photographic publishing company in the world, with over 2,000 sales outlets, and pioneered the picture postcard.

Francis Frith had died in 1898 at his villa in Cannes, his great project still growing. By 1970 the archive he created contained over a third of a million pictures showing 7,000 British towns and villages.

Frith's legacy to us today is of immense significance and value, for the magnificent archive of evocative photographs he created provides a unique record of change in the cities, towns and villages throughout Britain over a century and more. Frith and his fellow studio photographers revisited locations many times down the years to update their views, compiling for us an enthralling and colourful pageant of British life and character.

We are fortunate that Frith was dedicated to recording the minutiae of everyday life. For it is this sheer wealth of visual data, the painstaking chronicle of changes in dress, transport, street layouts, buildings, housing and landscape that captivates us so much today, offering us a powerful link with the past and with the lives of our ancestors.

Computers have now made it possible for Frith's many thousands of images to be accessed almost instantly. The archive offers every one of us an opportunity to examine the places where we and our families have lived and worked down the years. Its images, depicting our shared past, are now bringing pleasure and enlightenment to millions around the world a century and more after his death. For further information visit: www.francisfrith.co.uk

FREE PRINT OF YOUR CHOICE

Mounted Print
Overall size 14 x 11 inches (355 x 280mm)

**Choose any Frith photograph in this book.
Please note: photographs with a reference
number starting with a "Z" are not Frith
photographs and cannot be supplied under
this offer.**

Simply complete the Voucher opposite and
return it with your remittance for £2.25 (to cover
postage and handling) and we will print the
photograph of your choice in SEPIA (size 11 x 8
inches) and supply it in a cream mount with a
burgundy rule line (overall size 14 x 11 inches).
Offer valid for delivery to one UK address only.

**PLUS: Order additional Mounted Prints
at HALF PRICE - £7.49 each** (normally £14.99)
If you would like to order more Frith prints from
this book, possibly as gifts for friends and family,
you can buy them at half price (with no
additional postage and handling costs).

PLUS: Have your Mounted Prints framed
For an extra £14.95 per print you can have your
mounted print(s) framed in an elegant polished wood and gilt moulding, overall size 16 x
13 inches (no additional postage and handling
required).

IMPORTANT!

**These special prices are only available if you use
this form to order. You must use the ORIGINAL
VOUCHER on this page (no copies permitted). We
can only despatch to one UK address. This offer
cannot be combined with any other offer.**

Send completed Voucher form to:
**The Francis Frith Collection, Frith's Barn,
Teffont, Salisbury, Wiltshire SP3 5QP**

CHOOSE A PHOTOGRAPH FROM THIS BOOK

Voucher for FREE and Reduced Price Frith Prints

*Please do not photocopy this voucher. Only the original is valid,
so please fill it in, cut it out and return it to us with your order.*

Picture ref no	Page no	Qty	Mounted @ £7.49	Framed + £14.95	Total Cost £
		1	Free of charge*	£	£
			£7.49	£	£
			£7.49	£	£
			£7.49	£	£
			£7.49	£	£
			£7.49	£	£

*Please allow 28 days for delivery.
Offer available to one UK address only*

* Post & handling	£2.25
Total Order Cost	£

Title of this book . . . .

I enclose a cheque/postal order for £ . . . .
made payable to 'The Francis Frith Collection'

OR please debit my Mastercard / Visa / Maestro card,
details below

Card Number

Issue No (Maestro only)   Valid from (Maestro)

Expires   Signature

Name Mr/Mrs/Ms . . . .
Address . . . .
. . . .
. . . .
. . . . Postcode . . . .
Daytime Tel No . . . .
Email . . . .

ISBN: 1-84589-208-9   Valid to 31/12/08

CAN YOU HELP US WITH INFORMATION ABOUT ANY OF THE FRITH PHOTOGRAPHS IN THIS BOOK?

We are gradually compiling an historical record for each of the photographs in the Frith archive. It is always fascinating to find out the names of the people shown in the pictures, as well as insights into the shops, buildings and other features depicted.

If you recognize anyone in the photographs in this book, or if you have information not already included in the author's caption, do let us know. We would love to hear from you, and will try to publish it in future books or articles.

OUR PRODUCTION TEAM

Frith books are produced by a small dedicated team at offices in the converted Grade II listed 18th-century barn at Teffont near Salisbury, illustrated above. Most have worked with the Frith Collection for many years. All have in common one quality: they have a passion for the Frith Collection. The team is constantly expanding, but currently includes:

Paul Baron, Jason Buck, John Buck, Heather Crisp, David Davies, Louis du Mont, Isobel Hall, Lucy Hart, Julian Hight, Peter Horne, James Kinnear, Karen Kinnear, Tina Leary, Stuart Login, Sue Molloy, Miles Murray, Sarah Roberts, Kate Rotondetto, Dean Scource, Eliza Sackett, Terence Sackett, Sandra Sampson, Adrian Sanders, Sandra Sanger, Julia Skinner, Lewis Taylor, Shelley Tolcher, Lorraine Tuck, Miranda Tunnicliffe, David Turner and Ricky Williams.